YOUR PERSONAL
HOROSCOPE
2008

CANCER

YOUR PERSONAL
HOROSCOPE
2008

CANCER
22nd June–22nd July

igloo

igloo

This edition published by Igloo Books Ltd,
Cottage Farm, Mears Ashby Road, Sywell, Northants NN6 0BJ
www.igloo-books.com
E-mail: Info@igloo-books.com

Produced for Igloo Books by W. Foulsham & Co. Ltd,
The Publishing House, Bennetts Close, Cippenham,
Slough, Berkshire SL1 5AP, England

ISBN: 978-1-845-61610-6

This is an abridged version of material
originally published in *Old Moore's Horoscope
and Astral Diary*.

Printed in China

CONTENTS

CONTENTS

INTRODUCTION

Your Personal Horoscopes have been specifically created to allow you to get the most from astrological patterns and the way they have a bearing on not only your zodiac sign, but nuances within it. Using the diary section of the book you can read about the influences and possibilities of each and every day of the year. It will be possible for you to see when you are likely to be cheerful and happy or those times when your nature is in retreat and you will be more circumspect. The diary will help to give you a feel for the specific 'cycles' of astrology and the way they can subtly change your day-to-day life. For example, when you see the sign ☿, this means that the planet Mercury is retrograde at that time. Retrograde means it appears to be running backwards through the zodiac. Such a happening has a significant effect on communication skills, but this is only one small aspect of how the Personal Horoscope can help you.

With Your Personal Horoscope the story doesn't end with the diary pages. It includes simple ways for you to work out the zodiac sign the Moon occupied at the time of your birth, and what this means for your personality. In addition, if you know the time of day you were born, it is possible to discover your Ascendant, yet another important guide to your personal make-up and potential.

Many readers are interested in relationships and in knowing how well they get on with people of other astrological signs. You might also be interested in the way you appear to very different sorts of individuals. If you are such a person, the section on Venus will be of particular interest. Despite the rapidly changing position of this planet, you can work out your Venus sign, and learn what bearing it will have on your life.

Using Your Personal Horoscope you can travel on one of the most fascinating and rewarding journeys that anyone can take – the journey to a better realisation of self.

THE ESSENCE
OF CANCER

Exploring the Personality of Cancer the Crab

(22ND JUNE – 22ND JULY)

What's in a sign?

The most obvious fact about you, particularly when viewed by others, is that you are trustworthy. Sometimes this fact gets on your nerves. Many Cancerians long to be bigger, bolder and more ruthless, but it simply isn't the way you were made. You are basically ruled by your emotions and there is very little you can do to get away from the fact. Once you realise this you could be in for a happy life but there are bound to be some frustrations on the way.

Your ruling planet is the Moon, which changes its position in astrological terms far more quickly than any other heavenly body. That's why you can sometimes feel that you have experienced a whole year's emotions in only a month. However the saving grace of this fact is that unlike the other Water signs of Scorpio and Pisces, you are rarely bogged down by emotional restraints for more than a day or two at a time. This gives you a more optimistic attitude and a determination to use your natural talents to the full, even in the face of some adversity. Caring for others is second nature to you and forms a very large part of your life and character.

Your attitude towards romance fluctuates but is generally of the 'story book' sort. Once you commit yourself to another person, either romantically or practically, you are not likely to change your mind very easily. Loyalty is part of what you are about and doesn't change just because things sometimes get a little complicated. Even when you don't really know where you are going, you are inclined to pull those you love along the path with you, and you can usually rely on their assistance. Basically you are very easy to love and there can't be anything much wrong with that fact. At the same time you can be very practical, don't mind doing some of the dirty work and are in your element when those around you are floundering.

The creative potential within your nature is strong. You are a natural homemaker and tend to get a great deal from simply watching others succeed. All the same this isn't the whole story because you are complex and inclined to be too worrisome.

Cancer resources

Your ruling planet is the Moon, Earth's closest neighbour in space. This means that you are as subject to its tides and fluctuations as is our planet. Of course this is a double-edged sword because you can sometimes be an emotional maelstrom inside. To compensate for this fact you have a level of personal sensitivity that would be admired by many. At the same time you have a deep intuition and can usually be relied upon to see through the mist of everyday life and to work out how situations are likely to mature. This is especially true when it comes to assessing those around you.

As a homemaker you are second to none. You can make a few pounds go a very long way and can cope well in circumstances that would greatly trouble those around you. Adversity is not something that bothers you too much at all and it is clear that you can even revel in difficulty. Nothing is too much trouble when you are dealing with people you really love – which includes friends as well as family members.

One of the greatest Cancerian resources is the ability to bring a practical face to even difficult circumstances. Physically speaking you are very resilient, even if you don't always seem to be the strongest person around in an emotional sense. You are given to showing extreme kindness, sometimes even in the face of cruelty from others, though if you are genuinely provoked you can show an anger that would shock most people, even those who think they know you very well indeed.

What really counts the most is your ability to bring others round to your point of view and to get them to do what you think is best. Working from example you won't generally expect others to do anything you are not prepared to try yourself, and your attitude can be an inspiration to others. Through hard work and perseverance you can build a good life for yourself, though your consideration for those around you never diminishes and so even a fortune gained would generally be used on behalf of the world around you. The greatest resource that you possess is your capacity to love and to nurture. This makes you successful and well loved by others.

Beneath the surface

The most difficult aspect of those born under the sign of Cancer the Crab is trying to work out the psychological motivations of this apparently simple but actually deeply complex zodiac position. 'Emotion' is clearly the keyword and is the fountain from which everything, good and bad alike, flows. Whilst some zodiac sign types are inclined to act and then consider the consequences, the Crab is a different beast altogether. The main quality of Cancer is caring. This applies as much to the world at large as it does in consideration of family, though to the Crab it's clear that under almost all circumstances family comes first.

You are a deep thinker and don't always find it easy to explain the way your mind is working. The reason for this is not so difficult to understand. Feelings are not the same as thoughts and it is sometimes quite difficult to express the qualities that rule you internally. What you seem to prefer to do is to put a caring arm around the world and express your inner compassion in this manner. You might also sometimes be a little anxious that if others knew how your innermost mind worked you would become more vulnerable than you already are – which is why the Crab wears a shell in the first place.

At the first sign of emotional pressure from outside you are inclined to retreat into yourself. As a result you don't always confront issues that would be best dealt with immediately. This proclivity runs deep and strong in your nature and can sometimes cause you much more trouble than would be the case if you just made the right statements and asked the correct questions. Physically and mentally you are not inclined to withdraw because you are very much stronger than the world would give you credit for.

Cancerians have a tremendous capacity to love, allied to a potential for positive action when the lives or well-being of others is threatened. In some ways you are the bravest zodiac sign of all because you will march forward into the very gates of hell if you know that you can be of service to those around you. From family to village or town, from town to nation and from nation to a global awareness, yours is the zodiac sign that best epitomises humanity's struggle for a universal understanding.

Making the best of yourself

If you start out from the premise that you are well liked by most people then you are halfway towards any intended destination. Of course you don't always register your popularity and are given to worrying about the impression you give. The picture you paint of yourself is usually very different from the one the world at large sees. If you doubt this, ask some of your best friends to describe your nature and you will be quite surprised. You need to be as open as possible to avoid internalising matters that would be best brought into a more public arena. Your natural tendency to look after everyone else masks a desire to get on in life personally, and the Cancerians who succeed the best are the ones who have somehow managed to bring a sense of balance to their giving and taking.

Try to avoid being too quiet. In social situations you have much to offer, though would rarely do so in a particularly gregarious manner. Nevertheless, and partly because you don't shoot your mouth off all the time, people are willing to listen to what you have to say. Once you realise how strong your influence can be you are already on the road to riches – financial and personal.

Use your imagination to the full because it is one of the most potent weapons in your personal armoury. People won't underestimate you when they know how strong you really are and that means that life can sometimes be less of a struggle. But under most circumstances be your usual warm self, and the love you desire will come your way.

The very practical issues of life are easy for you to deal with, which is why your material success is generally assured. All that is needed to make the picture complete is more confidence in your ability to lead and less inclination to follow.

The impressions you give

There is no doubt at all that you are one of the most loved and the most admired people around. It isn't hard to see why. Your relatives and friends alike feel very protected and loved, which has got to be a good start when it comes to your contacts with the world at large. The most intriguing thing about being a Cancerian subject is how different you appear to be when viewed by others as against the way you judge your own personality. This is down to external appearances as much as anything. For starters you usually wear a cheery smile, even on those occasions when it is clear you are not smiling inside. You give yourself fully to the needs and wants of those around you and are very sympathetic, even towards strangers. It's true that you may not fully exploit the implications of your pleasant nature – but that's only another typical part of your character.

Those people who know you the best are aware that you have a great capacity to worry about things, and they may also understand that you are rarely as confident as you give the external impression of being. They sense the deeply emotional quality of your nature and can observe the long periods of deep thought. When it comes to the practicalities of life, however, you perhaps should not be surprised that you are sometimes put on rather too much. Even this is understandable because you rarely say no and will usually make yourself available when there is work to be done.

True success for the Cancer subject lies in recognising your strong points and in being willing to gain from them in a personal sense from time to time. You also need to realise that, to others, the impression you give is what you really are. Bridging the gap between outward calm and inner confusion might be the most important lesson.

The way forward

Although you don't always feel quite as sure of yourself as you give the impression of being, you can still exploit your external appearance to your own and other people's advantage. Your strong sense of commitment to family and your ability to get on well in personal relationships are both factors that improve your ability to progress in life.

Achieving a sense of balance is important. For example you can spend long hours locked into your own thoughts, but this isn't good for you in an exclusive sense. Playing out some of your fantasies in the real world can do you good, even though you are aware that this involves taking chances, something you don't always care to do. At the same time you should not be afraid to make gains as a result of the way you are loved by others. This doesn't come for free and you work long and hard to establish the affection that comes your way.

In practical matters you are capable and well able to get on in life. Money comes your way, not usually as a result of particularly good luck, but because you are a tireless and steady worker. You can accept responsibility, even though the implied management side of things worries you somewhat. To have a career is important because it broadens your outlook and keeps you functioning in the wider world, which is where your personal successes take place. The more you achieve, the greater is the level of confidence that you feel – which in turn leads to even greater progress.

Cancerians should never cut themselves off from the mainstream of life. It's true you have many acquaintances but very few really close friends, but that doesn't matter. Practically everyone you know is pleased to name you as a trusted ally, which has to be the best compliment of all to your apparently serene and settled nature.

In love you are ardent and sincere. It may take you a while to get round to expressing the way you feel, partly because you are a little afraid of failure in this most important area of your life. All the same you love with a passion and are supportive to your partner. Family will always be the most important sphere of life because your zodiac sign rules the astrological fourth house, which is essentially dedicated to home and family matters. If you are contented in this arena it tends to show in other areas of your life too. Your affable nature is your best friend and only tends to disappear if you allow yourself to become too stressed.

CANCER ON THE CUSP

Astrological profiles are altered for those people born at either the beginning or the end of a zodiac sign, or, more properly, on the cusps of a sign. In the case of Cancer this would be on the 22nd of June and for two or three days after, and similarly at the end of the sign, probably from the 20th to the 22nd of July.

The Gemini Cusp – June 22nd to June 24th

You are certainly fun to be around and the sign of Gemini has a great deal to do with your basic motivations. As a result, you tend to be slightly more chatty than the average Cancerian and usually prove to be the life and soul of any party that is going on in your vicinity. Not everyone understands the basic sensitivity that lies below the surface of this rather brash exterior, however, and you can sometimes be a little hurt if people take you absolutely at face value. There probably isn't the total consistency of emotional responses that one generally expects to find in the Crab when taken alone, and there are times when you might be accused of being rather fickle. All the same, you have a big heart and show genuine concern for anyone in trouble, especially the underdog. Your Gemini attributes give you the opportunity to speak your mind, so when it comes to aiding the world you can be a tireless reformer and show a great ability to think before you speak, which is not typical of Gemini on its own, although there are occasions when the two sides of your nature tend to be at odds with each other.

At work you are very capable and can be relied upon to make instant decisions whenever necessary. Your executive capabilities are pronounced and you are more than capable of thinking on your feet, even if you prefer to mull things over if possible. You are the sort of person that others tend to rely on for advice and will not usually let your colleagues or friends down.

In matters of love, you are less steadfast and loyal than the Crab, yet you care very deeply for your loved ones. People like to have you around and actively seek your advice which, in the main, is considered and sound, though always delivered with humour. You love to travel and would never wish to be limited in either your horizons or your lifestyle. All in all, you are a fun person, good to know, and basically sensible.

The Leo Cusp – July 20th to July 22nd

Here we find a Cancerian who tends to know what he or she want from life. Part of the natural tendency of the Crab is to be fairly sh and retiring, though progressively less so as the Sun moves o towards the sign of Leo. You are probably aware that you don' exactly match the Cancer stereotype and are likely to be mor outspoken, determined and even argumentative at times. You hav lofty ideals, which find a ready home for the sensitive qualities tha you draw from Cancer. Many social reformers tend to have thei Suns very close to the Leo cusp of Cancer and people born on thi cusp like to work hard for the world, especially for the less well-of members of society.

In matters of love, you are deep, but ardent and sincere, findin better ways of expressing your emotions verbally than thos generally associated with the Crab. You are capable at work, easil able to take on responsibilities that involve controlling other peopl and you are outwardly braver than often seems to be the case wit Cancer alone. Not everyone finds you particularly easy t understand, probably because there are some definite paradoxe about your nature.

A few problems come along in the area of ideals, which are mor important to you than they would be to some of the people wit whom you associate. You need to be sure of yourself, a fact tha leads to fairly long thinking periods, but once you have formed particular belief you will move heaven and earth to demonstrat how sensible it is. Don't be too alarmed if not everyone agree with you.

You are not the typical conformist that might more usually b the case with Cancerians, and feel the need to exercise your civi rights to the full. Tireless when dealing with something you think i especially important, you are a good and loyal friend, a staunch an steadfast lover and you care deeply about your family. However, yo are not as confrontational as a person born completely under Leo and therefore can usually be relied upon to seek a compromise.

CANCER AND ITS ASCENDANTS

The nature of every individual on the planet is composed of the rich variety of zodiac signs and planetary positions that were present at the time of their birth. Your Sun sign, which in your case is Cancer, is one of the many factors when it comes to assessing the unique person you are. Probably the most important consideration, other than your Sun sign, is to establish the zodiac sign that was rising over the eastern horizon at the time that you were born. This is your Ascending or Rising sign. Most popular astrology fails to take account of the Ascendant, and yet its importance remains with you from the very moment of your birth, through every day of your life. The Ascendant is evident in the way you approach the world, and so, when meeting a person for the first time, it is this astrological influence that you are most likely to notice first. Our Ascending sign essentially represents what we appear to be, while the Sun sign is what we feel inside ourselves.

The Ascendant also has the potential for modifying our overall nature. For example, if you were born at a time of day when Cancer was passing over the eastern horizon (this would be around the time of dawn) then you would be classed as a double Cancerian. As such, you would typify this zodiac sign, both internally and in your dealings with others. However, if your Ascendant sign turned out to be a Fire sign, such as Aries, there would be a profound alteration of nature, away from the expected qualities of Cancer.

One of the reasons why popular astrology often ignores the Ascendant is that it has always been rather difficult to establish. We have found a way to make this possible by devising an easy-to-use table, which you will find on page 157 of this book. Using this, you can establish your Ascendant sign at a glance. You will need to know your rough time of birth, then it is simply a case of following the instructions.

For those readers who have no idea of their time of birth it might be worth allowing a good friend, or perhaps your partner, to read through the section that follows this introduction. Someone who deals with you on a regular basis may easily discover your Ascending sign, even though you could have some difficulty establishing it for yourself. A good understanding of this component of your nature is essential if you want to be aware of that 'other person' who is responsible for the way you make contact

17

with the world at large. Your Sun sign, Ascendant sign, and the other pointers in this book will, together, allow you a far better understanding of what makes you tick as an individual. Peeling back the different layers of your astrological make-up can be an enlightening experience, and the Ascendant may represent one of the most important layers of all.

Cancer with Cancer Ascendant

You are one of the most warm and loving individuals that it is possible to know, and you carry a quiet dignity that few would fail to recognise. Getting on with things in your own steady way, you are, nevertheless, capable of great things, simply because you keep going. Even in the face of adversity your steady but relentless pace can be observed, and much of what you do is undertaken on behalf of those you love the most. On the other side of the coin you represent something of a mystery and it is also true that emotionally speaking you tend to be very highly charged. It doesn't take much to bring you to tears and you are inclined to have a special affection for the underdog, which on occasions can get you into a little trouble. Although it is your natural way to keep a low profile, you will speak out loudly if you think that anyone you care for is under attack, and yet you don't show the same tendency on your own behalf.

Rarely if ever out of control, you are the levelling influence everyone feels they need in their life, which is one of the reasons why you are so loved. Your quiet ways are accepted by the world which is why some people will be astonished when you suddenly announce that you are about to travel overland to Asia. What a great puzzle you can be, but that is half the attraction.

Cancer with Leo Ascendant

This can be a very fortunate combination, for when seen at its best it brings all the concern and the natural caring qualities of Cancer, allied to the more dynamic and very brave face of Leo. Somehow there is a great deal of visible energy here, but it manifests itself in a way that always shows a concern for the world at large. No matter what charitable works are going on in your district it is likely that you will be involved in one way or another, and you relish the cut and thrust of life much more than the the retiring side of Cancer would seem to do. You are quite capable of walking alone and don't really need the company of others for large chunks of the average day. However, when you are in social situations you fare very well and can usually be observed with a smile on your face.

Conversationally speaking you have sound, considered opinions and often represent the voice of steady wisdom when faced with a situation that means arbitration. In fact you will often be put in this situation, and there is more than one politician and union representative who shares this undeniably powerful zodiac combination. Like all those associated with the sign of Cancer you love to travel and can make a meal out of your journeys with brave, intrepid Leo lending a hand in both the planning and the doing.

Cancer with Virgo Ascendant

What can this union of zodiac signs bring to the party that isn't there in either Cancer or Virgo alone? Well, quite a bit actually. Virgo can be very fussy on occasions and too careful for its own good. The presence of steady, serene Cancer alters the perspective and allows a smoother, more flowing individual to greet the world. You are chatty and easy to know, and exhibit a combination of the practical skills of Virgo, together with the deep and penetrating insights that are typical of Cancer. This can make you appear to be very powerful and your insights are second to none. You are a born organiser and love to be where things are happening, even if you are only there to help make the sandwiches or to pour the tea. Invariably your role will be much greater but you don't seek personal acclaim and are a good team player on most occasions.

There is a quiet side to your nature and those who live with you will eventually get used to your need for solitude. This seems strange because Virgo is generally such a chatterbox and, taken on its own, is rarely quiet for long. In matters of love you show great affection and a sense of responsibility that makes you an ideal parent. It is sometimes the case, however, that you care rather more than you should be willing to show.

Cancer with Libra Ascendant

What an absolutely pleasant and approachable sort of person you are, and how much you have to offer. Like most people associated with the sign of Cancer, you give yourself freely to the world and will always be on hand if anyone is in trouble or needs the special touch you can bring to almost any problem. Behaving in this way is the biggest part of what you are and so people come to rely on you very heavily. Like Libra you can see both sides of any coin and you exhibit the Libran tendency to jump about from one foot to the other when it is necessary to make decisions relating to your own life. This is not usually the case when you are dealing with others, however, because the cooler and more detached qualities of Cancer will show through in these circumstances.

It would be fair to say that you do not deal with routines as well as Cancer alone might do and you need a degree of variety in your life. In your case this possibly comes in the form of travel, which can be distant and of long duration. It isn't unusual for people who have this zodiac combination to end up living abroad, though even this does little to prevent you from getting itchy feet from time to time. In relationships you show an original quality that keeps the relationship young, fresh and working well.

Cancer with Scorpio Ascendant

There are few more endearing zodiac combinations than this. Both signs are Watery in nature and show a desire to work on behalf of humanity as a whole. The world sees you as being genuinely caring, full of sympathy for anyone in trouble and always ready to lend a hand when it is needed. You are a loyal friend, a great supporter of the oppressed and a lover of home and family. In a work sense you are capable and command respect from your colleagues, even though this comes about courtesy of your quiet competence, and not as a result of anything that you might happen to say or do.

But we should not get too carried away with external factors, or the way that others see you. Inside you are a boiling pool of emotion. You feel more strongly, love more deeply and hurt more fully than any other combination of the Water signs. Even those who think that they know you really well would get a shock if they could take a stroll around the deeper recesses of your mind. Although these facts are true, they may be rather beside the point because the truth of your passion, commitment and deep convictions may only surface fully half a dozen times in your life. The fact is that you are a very private person at heart and you don't know how to be any other way.

Cancer with Sagittarius Ascendant

You have far more drive, enthusiasm and get-up-and-go than would seem to be the case for Cancer when taken alone, but all of this is tempered with a certain quiet compassion that probably makes you the best sort of Sagittarian too. It's true that you don't like to be on your own or to retire into your shell quite as much as the Crab usually does, though there are, even in your case, occasions when this is going to be necessary. Absolute concentration can sometimes be a problem to you, though this is hardly likely to be the case when you are dealing with matters relating to your home or family, both of which reign supreme in your thinking. Always loving and kind, you are a social animal and enjoy being out there in the real world, expressing the deeper opinions of Cancer much more readily than would often be the case with other combinations relating to the sign of the Crab.

Personality is not lacking, and you tend to be very popular, not least because you are the fountain of good and practical advice. You want to get things done, and retain a practical approach to most situations which is the envy of many of the people you meet. As a parent you are second to none, combining common sense, dignity and a sensible approach. To balance this you stay young enough to understand children.

Cancer with Capricorn Ascendant

The single most important factor here is the practical ability to get things done and to see any task, professional or personal, through to the end. Since half this combination is Cancer, that also means expounding much of your energy on behalf of others. There isn't a charity in the world that would fail to recognise what a potent combination this is when it comes to the very concrete side of offering help and assistance. Many of your ideas hold water and you don't set off on abortive journeys of any kind, simply because you tend to get the ground rules fixed in your mind first.

On a more personal level you can be rather hard to get to know, because both these signs have a deep quality and a tendency to keep things in the dark. The mystery may only serve to encourage people to try and get to know you better. As a result you could attract a host of admirers, many of whom would wish to form romantic attachments. This may prove to be irrelevant, however, because once you give your heart, you tend to be loyal and would only change your mind if you were pushed into doing so. Prolonged periods of inactivity don't do you any good and it is sensible for you to keep on the move, even though your progress in life is measured and very steady.

Cancer with Aquarius Ascendant

The truly original spark, for which the sign of Aquarius is famed, can only enhance the caring qualities of Cancer, and is also inclined to bring the Crab out of its shell to a much greater extent than would be the case with certain other zodiac combinations. Aquarius is a party animal and never arrives without something interesting to say, which is doubly so when the reservoir of emotion and consideration that is Cancer is feeding the tap. Your nature can be rather confusing, even for you to deal with, but you are inspirational, bright, charming and definitely fun to be around.

The Cancer element in your nature means that you care about your home and the people to whom you are related. You are also a good and loyal friend, who would keep attachments for much longer than could be expected for Aquarius alone. You love to travel and can be expected to make many journeys to far-off places during your life. Some attention will have to be paid to your health because you are capable of burning up masses of nervous energy, often without getting the periods of rest and contemplation that are essential to the deeper qualities of the sign of Cancer. Nevertheless you have determination, resilience and a refreshing attitude that lifts the spirits of the people in your vicinity.

Cancer with Pisces Ascendant

A deep, double Water-sign combination, this one, and it migh serve to make you a very misunderstood, though undoubtedl popular, individual. You are keen to make a good impression probably too keen under certain circumstances, and you d everything you can to help others, even if you don't know them very well. It's true that you are deeply sensitive and quite easil brought to tears by the suffering of this most imperfect world tha we inhabit. Fatigue can be a problem, though this is nullified t some extent by the fact that you can withdraw completely int the deep recesses of your own mind when it becomes necessary t do so.

You may not be the most gregarious person in the world, simpl because it isn't easy for you to put your most importan considerations into words. This is easier when you are in th company of people you know and trust, though even trust is commodity that is difficult for you to find, particularly since yo may have been hurt by being too willing to share your thought early in life. With age comes wisdom and maturity and the older yo are, the better you will learn to handle this potent and demandin combination. You will never go short of either friends or would-b lovers, and may be one of the most magnetic types of both Canc and Pisces.

Cancer with Aries Ascendant

The main problem that you experience in life shows itself as a direct result of the meshing of these two very different zodiac signs. At heart Aries needs to dominate, whereas Cancer shows a desire to nurture. All too often the result can be a protective arm that is so strong that nobody could possibly get out from under it. Lighten your own load, and that of those you care for, by being willing to sit back and watch others please themselves a little. You might think that you know best, and your heart is clearly in the right place, but try and realise what life can be like when someone is always on hand to tell you that they know better than you do.

But in a way this is a little severe, because you are fairly intuitive and your instincts will rarely lead you astray. Nobody could ask for a better partner or parent than you would be, though they might request a slightly less attentive one. In matters of work you are conscientious, and are probably best suited to a job that means sorting out the kind of mess that humanity is so good at creating. You probably spend your spare time untangling balls of wool, though you are quite sporting too and could even make the Olympics. Once there you would not win however, because you would be too concerned about all the other competitors!

Cancer with Taurus Ascendant

Your main aim in life seems to be to look after everyone and everything that you come across. From your deepest and most enduring human love, right down to the birds in the park, you really do care and you show that natural affection in many different ways. Your nature is sensitive and you are easily moved to tears, though this does not prevent you from pitching in and doing practical things to assist at just about any level. There is a danger that you could stifle those same people whom you set out to assist, and people with this zodiac combination are often unwilling, or unable, to allow their children to grow and leave the nest. More time spent considering what suits you would be no bad thing, but the problem is that you find it almost impossible to imagine any situation that doesn't involve your most basic need, which is to nurture.

You appear not to possess a selfish streak, though it sometimes turns out that in being certain that you understand the needs of the world, you are nevertheless treading on their toes. This eventual realisation can be very painful, but it isn't a stick with which you should beat yourself because at heart you are one of the kindest people imaginable. Your sense of fair play means that you are a quiet social reformer at heart.

Cancer with Gemini Ascendant

Many astrologers would say that this is a happy combination because some of the more flighty qualities of Gemini are somewhat modified by the steady influence of Cancer the Crab. To all intents and purposes you show the friendly and gregarious qualities of Gemini, but there is a thoughtful and even sometimes a serious quality that would not be present in Gemini when taken alone. Looking after people is high on your list of priorities and you do this most of the time. This is made possible because you have greater staying power than Gemini is usually said to possess and you can easily see fairly complicated situations through to their conclusion without becoming bored on the way.

The chances are that you will have many friends and that these people show great concern for your well-being, because you choose them carefully and show them a great deal of consideration. However, you will still be on the receiving end of gossip on occasions, and need to treat such situations with a healthy pinch of salt. Like all part-Geminis your nervous system is not as strong as you would wish to believe and family pressures in particular can put great strain on you. Activities of all kinds take your fancy and many people with this combination are attracted to sailing or wind surfing.

THE MOON AND THE PART IT PLAYS IN YOUR LIFE

In astrology the Moon is probably the single most important heavenly body after the Sun. Its unique position, as partner to the Earth on its journey around the solar system, means that the Moon appears to pass through the signs of the zodiac extremely quickly. The zodiac position of the Moon at the time of your birth plays a great part in personal character and is especially significant in the build-up of your emotional nature.

Your Own Moon Sign

Discovering the position of the Moon at the time of your birth has always been notoriously difficult because tracking the complex zodiac positions of the Moon is not easy. This process has been reduced to three simple stages with our Lunar Tables. A breakdown of the Moon's zodiac positions can be found from page 35 onwards, so that once you know what your Moon Sign is, you can see what part this plays in the overall build-up of your personal character.

If you follow the instructions on the next page you will soon be able to work out exactly what zodiac sign the Moon occupied on the day that you were born and you can then go on to compare the reading for this position with those of your Sun sign and your Ascendant. It is partly the comparison between these three important positions that goes towards making you the unique individual you are.

HOW TO DISCOVER YOUR MOON SIGN

This is a three-stage process. You may need a pen and a piece of paper but if you follow the instructions below the process should only take a minute or so.

STAGE 1 First of all you need to know the Moon Age at the time of your birth. If you look at Moon Table 1, on page 33, you will find all the years between 1910 and 2008 down the left side. Find the year of your birth and then trace across to the right to the month of your birth. Where the two intersect you will find a number. This is the date of the New Moon in the month that you were born. You now need to count forward the number of days between the New Moon and your own birthday. For example, if the New Moon in the month of your birth was shown as being the 6th and you were born on the 20th, your Moon Age Day would be 14. If the New Moon in the month of your birth came after your birthday, you need to count forward from the New Moon in the previous month. If you were born in a Leap Year, remember to count the 29th February. You can tell if your birth year was a Leap Year if the last two digits can be divided by four. Whatever the result, jot this number down so that you do not forget it.

STAGE 2 Take a look at Moon Table 2 on page 34. Down the left hand column look for the date of your birth. Now trace across to the month of your birth. Where the two meet you will find a letter. Copy this letter down alongside your Moon Age Day.

STAGE 3 Moon Table 3 on page 34 will supply you with the zodiac sign the Moon occupied on the day of your birth. Look for your Moon Age Day down the left hand column and then for the letter you found in Stage 2. Where the two converge you will find a zodiac sign and this is the sign occupied by the Moon on the day that you were born.

Your Zodiac Moon Sign Explained

You will find a profile of all zodiac Moon Signs on pages 35 to 38, showing in yet another way how astrology helps to make you into the individual that you are. In each daily entry of the Astral Diary you can find the zodiac position of the Moon for every day of the year. This also allows you to discover your lunar birthdays. Since the Moon passes through all the signs of the zodiac in about a month, you can expect something like twelve lunar birthdays each year. At these times you are likely to be emotionally steady and able to make the sort of decisions that have real, lasting value.

MOON TABLE 1

EAR	MAY	JUN	JUL	YEAR	MAY	JUN	JUL	YEAR	MAY	JUN	JUL
910	9	7	6	1943	4	2	2	1976	29	27	27
911	28	26	25	1944	22	20	20	1977	18	16	16
912	17	16	15	1945	11	10	9	1978	7	5	5
913	5	4	3	1946	1/30	29	28	1979	26	24	24
914	24	23	22	1947	19	18	17	1980	14	13	12
915	13	12	11	1948	9	7	6	1981	4	2	1/31
916	2	1/30	30	1949	27	26	25	1982	21	21	20
917	20	19	18	1950	17	15	15	1983	12	11	10
918	10	8	8	1951	6	4	4	1984	1/30	29	28
919	29	27	27	1952	23	22	22	1985	19	18	17
920	18	16	15	1953	13	11	11	1986	8	7	7
921	7	6	5	1954	2	1/30	29	1987	27	26	25
922	26	25	24	1955	21	20	19	1988	15	14	13
923	15	14	14	1956	10	8	8	1989	5	3	3
924	3	2	2/31	1957	29	27	27	1990	24	22	22
925	22	21	20	1958	18	17	16	1991	13	11	11
926	11	10	9	1959	7	6	6	1992	2	1/30	29
927	2/31	29	28	1960	26	24	24	1993	21	19	19
928	19	18	17	1961	14	13	12	1994	10	8	8
929	9	7	6	1962	4	2	1/31	1995	29	27	27
930	28	26	25	1963	23	21	20	1996	18	17	15
931	17	16	15	1964	11	10	9	1997	6	5	4
932	5	4	3	1965	1/30	29	28	1998	25	24	23
933	24	23	22	1966	19	18	17	1999	15	13	13
934	13	12	11	1967	8	7	7	2000	4	2	1/31
935	2	1/30	30	1968	27	26	25	2001	23	21	20
936	20	19	18	1969	15	14	13	2002	12	10	9
937	10	8	8	1970	6	4	4	2003	1/30	29	28
938	29	27	27	1971	24	22	22	2004	18	16	16
939	19	17	16	1972	13	11	11	2005	8	6	6
940	7	6	5	1973	2	1/30	29	2006	27	26	25
941	26	24	24	1974	21	20	19	2007	17	17	15
942	15	13	13	1975	11	9	9	2008	5	4	3

TABLE 2   MOON TABLE 3

DAY	JUN	JUL	M/D	O	P	Q	R	S	T	U
1	O	R	0	GE	GE	CA	CA	CA	LE	LE
2	P	R	1	GE	CA	CA	CA	LE	LE	LE
3	P	S	2	CA	CA	CA	LE	LE	LE	VI
4	P	S	3	CA	CA	LE	LE	LE	VI	VI
5	P	S	4	LE	LE	LE	LE	VI	VI	LI
6	P	S	5	LE	LE	VI	VI	VI	LI	LI
7	P	S	6	VI	VI	VI	VI	LI	LI	LI
8	P	S	7	VI	VI	LI	LI	LI	LI	SC
9	P	S	8	VI	VI	LI	LI	LI	SC	SC
10	P	S	9	LI	LI	SC	SC	SC	SC	SA
11	P	S	10	LI	LI	SC	SC	SC	SA	SA
12	Q	S	11	SC	SC	SC	SA	SA	SA	CP
13	Q	T	12	SC	SC	SA	SA	SA	SA	CP
14	Q	T	13	SC	SA	SA	SA	SA	CP	CP
15	Q	T	14	SA	SA	SA	CP	CP	CP	AQ
16	Q	T	15	SA	SA	CP	CP	CP	AQ	AQ
17	Q	T	16	CP	CP	CP	AQ	AQ	AQ	AQ
18	Q	T	17	CP	CP	CP	AQ	AQ	AQ	PI
19	Q	T	18	CP	CP	AQ	AQ	AQ	PI	PI
20	Q	T	19	AQ	AQ	AQ	PI	PI	PI	PI
21	Q	T	20	AQ	AQ	PI	PI	PI	AR	AR
22	R	T	21	AQ	PI	PI	PI	AR	AR	AR
23	R	T	22	PI	PI	PI	AR	AR	AR	TA
24	R	U	23	PI	PI	AR	AR	AR	TA	TA
25	R	U	24	PI	AR	AR	AR	TA	TA	TA
26	R	U	25	AR	AR	TA	TA	TA	GE	GE
27	R	U	26	AR	TA	TA	TA	GE	GE	GE
28	R	U	27	TA	TA	TA	GE	GE	GE	CA
29	R	U	28	TA	TA	GE	GE	GE	CA	CA
30	R	U	29	TA	GE	GE	GE	CA	CA	CA
31	–	U								

AR = Aries, TA = Taurus, GE = Gemini, CA = Cancer, LE = Leo, VI = Virgo
LI = Libra, SC = Scorpio, SA = Sagittarius, CP = Capricorn, AQ = Aquarius, PI = Pisce

MOON SIGNS

Moon in Aries

You have a strong imagination, courage, determination and a desire to do things in your own way and forge your own path through life.

Originality is a key attribute; you are seldom stuck for ideas although your mind is changeable and you could take the time to focus on individual tasks. Often quick-tempered, you take orders from few people and live life at a fast pace. Avoid health problems by taking regular time out for rest and relaxation.

Emotionally, it is important that you talk to those you are closest to and work out your true feelings. Once you discover that people are there to help, there is less necessity for you to do everything yourself.

Moon in Taurus

The Moon in Taurus gives you a courteous and friendly manner, which means you are likely to have many friends.

The good things in life mean a lot to you, as Taurus is an Earth sign that delights in experiences which please the senses. Hence you are probably a lover of good food and drink, which may in turn mean you need to keep an eye on the bathroom scales, especially as looking good is also important to you.

Emotionally you are fairly stable and you stick by your own standards. Taureans do not respond well to change. Intuition also plays an important part in your life.

Moon in Gemini

You have a warm-hearted character, sympathetic and eager to help others. At times reserved, you can also be articulate and chatty: this is part of the paradox of Gemini, which always brings duplicity to the nature. You are interested in current affairs, have a good intellect, and are good company and likely to have many friends. Most of your friends have a high opinion of you and would be ready to defend you should the need arise. However, this is usually unnecessary, as you are quite capable of defending yourself in any verbal confrontation.

Travel is important to your inquisitive mind and you find intellectual stimulus in mixing with people from different cultures. You also gain much from reading, writing and the arts but you do need plenty of rest and relaxation in order to avoid fatigue.

Moon in Cancer

The Moon in Cancer at the time of birth is a fortunate position a Cancer is the Moon's natural home. This means that the qualities o compassion and understanding given by the Moon are especiall enhanced in your nature, and you are friendly and sociable and cop well with emotional pressures. You cherish home and family life and happily do the domestic tasks. Your surroundings are importan to you and you hate squalor and filth. You are likely to have a love of music and poetry.

Your basic character, although at times changeable like th Moon itself, depends on symmetry. You aim to make you surroundings comfortable and harmonious, for yourself and thos close to you.

Moon in Leo

The best qualities of the Moon and Leo come together to make yo warm-hearted, fair, ambitious and self-confident. With good organisational abilities, you invariably rise to a position o responsibility in your chosen career. This is fortunate as you don' enjoy being an 'also-ran' and would rather be an important part o a small organisation than a menial in a large one.

You should be lucky in love, and happy, provided you put in th effort to make a comfortable home for yourself and those close to you. It is likely that you will have a love of pleasure, sport, musi and literature. Life brings you many rewards, most of them as a direct result of your own efforts, although you may be luckier than average and ready to make the best of any situation.

Moon in Virgo

You are endowed with good mental abilities and a keen receptive memory, but you are never ostentatious or pretentious. Naturall quite reserved, you still have many friends, especially of the opposite sex. Marital relationships must be discussed carefully and worked a so that they remain harmonious, as personal attachments can be a problem if you do not give them your full attention.

Talented and persevering, you possess artistic qualities and are a good homemaker. Earning your honours through genuine merit you work long and hard towards your objectives but show little pride in your achievements. Many short journeys will be undertaken in your life.

Moon in Libra

With the Moon in Libra you are naturally popular and make friends easily. People like you, probably more than you realise, you bring fun to a party and are a natural diplomat. For all its good points, Libra is not the most stable of astrological signs and, as a result, your emotions can be a little unstable too. Therefore, although the Moon in Libra is said to be good for love and marriage, your Sun sign and Rising sign will have an important effect on your emotional and loving qualities.

You must remember to relate to others in your decision-making. Co-operation is crucial because Libra represents the 'balance' of life that can only be achieved through harmonious relationships. Conformity is not easy for you because Libra, an Air sign, likes its independence.

Moon in Scorpio

Some people might call you pushy. In fact, all you really want to do is to live life to the full and protect yourself and your family from the pressures of life. Take care to avoid giving the impression of being sarcastic or impulsive and use your energies wisely and constructively.

You have great courage and you invariably achieve your goals by force of personality and sheer effort. You are fond of mystery and are good at predicting the outcome of situations and events. Travel experiences can be beneficial to you.

You may experience problems if you do not take time to examine your motives in a relationship, and also if you allow jealousy, always a feature of Scorpio, to cloud your judgement.

Moon in Sagittarius

The Moon in Sagittarius helps to make you a generous individual with humanitarian qualities and a kind heart. Restlessness may be intrinsic as your mind is seldom still. Perhaps because of this, you have a need for change that could lead you to several major moves during your adult life. You are not afraid to stand your ground when you know your judgement is right, you speak directly and have good intuition.

At work you are quick, efficient and versatile and so you make an ideal employee. You need work to be intellectually demanding and do not enjoy tedious routines.

In relationships, you anger quickly if faced with stupidity or deception, though you are just as quick to forgive and forget. Emotionally, there are times when your heart rules your head.

Moon in Capricorn

The Moon in Capricorn makes you popular and likely to come into the public eye in some way. The watery Moon is not entirely comfortable in the Earth sign of Capricorn and this may lead to some difficulties in the early years of life. An initial lack of creative ability and indecision must be overcome before the true qualities of patience and perseverance inherent in Capricorn can show through.

You have good administrative ability and are a capable worker, and if you are careful you can accumulate wealth. But you must be cautious and take professional advice in partnerships, as you are open to deception. You may be interested in social or welfare work, which suit your organisational skills and sympathy for others.

Moon in Aquarius

The Moon in Aquarius makes you an active and agreeable person with a friendly, easy-going nature. Sympathetic to the needs of others, you flourish in a laid-back atmosphere. You are broad-minded, fair and open to suggestion, although sometimes you have an unconventional quality which others can find hard to understand.

You are interested in the strange and curious, and in old articles and places. You enjoy trips to these places and gain much from them. Political, scientific and educational work interests you and you might choose a career in science or technology.

Money-wise, you make gains through innovation and concentration and Lunar Aquarians often tackle more than one job at a time. In love you are kind and honest.

Moon in Pisces

You have a kind, sympathetic nature, somewhat retiring at times, but you always take account of others' feelings and help when you can.

Personal relationships may be problematic, but as life goes on you can learn from your experiences and develop a better understanding of yourself and the world around you.

You have a fondness for travel, appreciate beauty and harmony and hate disorder and strife. You may be fond of literature and would make a good writer or speaker yourself. You have a creative imagination and may come across as an incurable romantic. You have strong intuition, maybe bordering on a mediumistic quality, which sets you apart from the mass. You may not be rich in cash terms, but your personal gifts are worth more than gold.

CANCER IN LOVE

Discover how compatible in love you are with people from the same and other signs of the zodiac. Five stars equals a match made in heaven!

Cancer meets Cancer

This match will work because the couple share a mutual understanding. Cancerians are very kind people who also respond well to kindness from others, so a double Cancer match can almost turn into a mutual appreciation society! But this will not lead to selfish hedonism, as the Crab takes in order to give more. There is an impressive physical, emotional and spiritual meeting of minds, which will lead to a successful and inspiring pairing in its own low-key and deeply sensitive way. Star rating: *****

Cancer meets Leo

This relationship will usually be directed by Leo more towards its own needs than Cancer's. However, the Crab will willingly play second fiddle to more progressive and bossy types as it is deeply emotional and naturally supportive. Leo is bright, caring, magnanimous and protective and so, as long as it isn't over-assertive, this could be a good match. On the surface, Cancer appears the more conventional of the two, but Leo will discover, to its delight, that it can be unusual and quirky. Star rating: ****

Cancer meets Virgo

This match has little chance of success, for fairly simple reasons: Cancer's generous affection will be submerged by the Virgoan depths, not because Virgo is uncaring but because it expresses itself so differently. As both signs are naturally quiet, things might become a bit boring. They would be mutually supportive, possibly financially successful and have a very tidy house, but they won't share much sparkle, enthusiasm, risk-taking or passion. If this pair were stranded on a desert island, they might live at different ends of it. Star rating: **

Cancer meets Libra

Almost anyone can get on with Libra, which is one of the most adaptable signs of them all. But being adaptable does not always lead to fulfilment, and a successful match here will require a quiet Libran and a slightly more progressive Cancerian than the norm. Both signs are pleasant, polite and like domestic order, but Libra may find Cancer too emotional and perhaps lacking in vibrancy, while Libra, on the other hand, may be a little too flighty for steady Cancer. Star rating: ***

Cancer meets Scorpio

This match is potentially a great success, a fact which is often a mystery to astrologers. Some feel it is due to the compatibility of the Water element, but it could also come from a mixture of similarity and difference in the personalities. Scorpio is partly ruled by Mars, which gives it a deep, passionate, dominant and powerful side. Cancerians generally like and respect this amalgam, and recognise something there that they would like to adopt themselves. On the other side of the coin, Scorpio needs love and emotional security which Cancer offers generously. Star rating: *****

Cancer meets Sagittarius

Although probably not an immediate success, there is hope for this couple. It's hard to see how this pair could get together, because they have few mutual interests. Sagittarius is always on the go, loves a hectic social life and dances the night away. Cancer prefers the cinema or a concert. But, having met, Cancer will appreciate the Archer's happy and cheerful nature, while Sagittarius finds Cancer alluring and intriguing and, as the saying goes, opposites attract. A long-term relationship would focus on commitment to family, with Cancer leading this area. Star rating: ***

Cancer meets Capricorn

Just about the only thing this pair have in common is the fact that both signs begin with 'Ca'! Some signs of the zodiac are instigators and some are reactors, and both the Crab and the Goat are reactors. Consequently, they both need incentives from their partners but won't find it in each other and, with neither side taking the initiative, there's a spark missing. Cancer and Capricorn do think alike in some ways and so, if they can find their spark or common purpose, they can be as happy as anyone. It's just rather unlikely. Star rating: **

Cancer meets Aquarius

Cancer is often attracted to Aquarius and, as Aquarius is automatically on the side of anyone who fancies it, so there is the potential for something good here. Cancer loves Aquarius' devil-may-care approach to life, but also recognises and seeks to strengthen the basic lack of self-confidence that all Air signs try so hard to keep secret. Both signs are natural travellers and are quite adventurous. Their family life would be unusual, even peculiar, but friends would recognise a caring, sharing household with many different interests shared by people genuinely in love. Star rating: ***

Cancer meets Pisces

This is likely to be a very successful match. Cancer and Pisces are both Water signs, and are both deep, sensitive and very caring. Pisces loves deeply, and Cancer wants to be loved. There will be few fireworks here, and a very quiet house. But that doesn't mean that either love or action is lacking – the latter of which is just behind closed doors. Family and children are important to both signs and both are prepared to work hard, but Pisces is the more restless of the two and needs the support and security that Cancer offers. Star rating: *****

Cancer meets Aries

A potentially one-sided pairing, it often appears that the Cancerian is brow-beaten by the far more dominant Arian. So much depends on the patience of the Cancerian individual, because if good psychology is present – who knows? But beware, Aries, you may find your partner too passive, and constantly having to take the lead can be wearing – even for you. A prolonged trial period would be advantageous, as the match could easily go either way. When it does work, though, this relationship is usually contented. Star rating: **

Cancer meets Taurus

This pair will have the tidiest house in the street – every stick of furniture in place, and no errant blade of grass daring to spoil the lawn. But things inside the relationship might not be quite so ship shape as both signs need, but don't offer, encouragement. There's plenty of affection, but few incentives for mutual progress. This might not prevent material success, but an enduring relationship isn't based on money alone. Passion is essential, and both parties need to realise and aim for that. Star rating: **

Cancer meets Gemini

This is often a very good match. Cancer is a very caring sign and quite adaptable. Geminis are untidy, have butterfly minds and are usually full of a thousand different schemes which Cancerians take in their stride and even relish. They can often be the 'wind beneath the wings' of their Gemini partners. In return, Gemini can eradicate some of the Cancerian emotional insecurity and will be more likely to be faithful in thought, word and deed to Cancer than to almost any other sign. Star rating: ****

VENUS:
THE PLANET OF LOVE

If you look up at the sky around sunset or sunrise you will often see Venus in close attendance to the Sun. It is arguably one of the most beautiful sights of all and there is little wonder that historically it became associated with the goddess of love. But although Venus does play an important part in the way you view love and in the way others see you romantically, this is only one of the spheres of influence that it enjoys in your overall character.

Venus has a part to play in the more cultured side of your life and has much to do with your appreciation of art, literature, music and general creativity. Even the way you look is responsive to the part of the zodiac that Venus occupied at the start of your life, though this fact is also down to your Sun sign and Ascending sign. If, at the time you were born, Venus occupied one of the more gregarious zodiac signs, you will be more likely to wear your heart on your sleeve, as well as to be more attracted to entertainment, social gatherings and good company. If on the other hand Venus occupied a quiet zodiac sign at the time of your birth, you would tend to be more retiring and less willing to shine in public situations.

It's good to know what part the planet Venus plays in your life for it can have a great bearing on the way you appear to the rest of the world and since we all have to mix with others, you can learn to make the very best of what Venus has to offer you.

One of the great complications in the past has always been trying to establish exactly what zodiac position Venus enjoyed when you were born because the planet is notoriously difficult to track. However, we have solved that problem by creating a table that is exclusive to your Sun sign, which you will find on the following page.

Establishing your Venus sign could not be easier. Just look up the year of your birth on the following page and you will see a sign of the zodiac. This was the sign that Venus occupied in the period covered by your sign in that year. If Venus occupied more than one sign during the period, this is indicated by the date on which the sign changed, and the name of the new sign. For instance, if you were born in 1950, Venus was in Taurus until the 27th June, after which time it was in Gemini. If you were born before 27th June your Venus sign is Taurus, if you were born on or after 27th June, your Venus sign is Gemini. Once you have established the position of Venus at the time of your birth, you can then look in the pages which follow to see how this has a bearing on your life as a whole.

1910 TAURUS / 30.6 GEMINI
1911 LEO / 7.7 VIRGO
1912 GEMINI / 25.6 CANCER / 19.7 LEO
1913 TAURUS / 8.7 GEMINI
1914 LEO / 16.7 VIRGO
1915 GEMINI / 11.7 CANCER
1916 CANCER
1917 CANCER / 5.7 LEO
1918 TAURUS / 29.6 GEMINI
1919 LEO / 8.7 VIRGO
1920 GEMINI / 25.6 CANCER / 18.7 LEO
1921 TAURUS / 8.7 GEMINI
1922 LEO / 15.7 VIRGO
1923 GEMINI / 10.7 CANCER
1924 CANCER
1925 CANCER / 4.7 LEO
1926 TAURUS / 28.6 GEMINI
1927 LEO / 8.7 VIRGO
1928 GEMINI / 24.6 CANCER / 18.7 LEO
1929 TAURUS / 8.7 GEMINI
1930 LEO / 15.7 VIRGO
1931 GEMINI / 10.7 CANCER
1932 CANCER
1933 CANCER / 4.7 LEO
1934 TAURUS / 27.6 GEMINI
1935 LEO / 8.7 VIRGO
1936 GEMINI / 24.6 CANCER / 17.7 LEO
1937 TAURUS / 8.7 GEMINI
1938 LEO / 14.7 VIRGO
1939 GEMINI / 9.7 CANCER
1940 CANCER / 13.7 GEMINI
1941 CANCER / 3.7 LEO
1942 TAURUS / 27.6 GEMINI
1943 LEO / 9.7 VIRGO
1944 GEMINI / 23.6 CANCER / 17.7 LEO
1945 TAURUS / 7.7 GEMINI
1946 LEO / 14.7 VIRGO
1947 GEMINI / 9.7 CANCER
1948 CANCER / 6.7 GEMINI
1949 CANCER / 2.7 LEO
1950 TAURUS / 27.6 GEMINI
1951 LEO / 9.7 VIRGO
1952 GEMINI / 23.6 CANCER / 17.7 LEO
1953 TAURUS / 7.7 GEMINI
1954 LEO / 13.7 VIRGO
1955 GEMINI / 8.7 CANCER
1956 CANCER / 29.6 GEMINI
1957 CANCER / 1.7 LEO
1958 TAURUS / 26.6 GEMINI

1959 LEO / 9.7 VIRGO
1960 CANCER / 16.7 LEO
1961 TAURUS / 7.7 GEMINI
1962 LEO / 13.7 VIRGO
1963 GEMINI / 8.7 CANCER
1964 CANCER / 22.6 GEMINI
1965 CANCER / 1.7 LEO
1966 TAURUS / 26.6 GEMINI
1967 LEO / 10.7 VIRGO
1968 CANCER / 16.7 LEO
1969 TAURUS / 6.7 GEMINI
1970 LEO / 13.7 VIRGO
1971 GEMINI / 7.7 CANCER
1972 CANCER / 22.6 GEMINI
1973 CANCER / 30.6 LEO
1974 TAURUS / 26.6 GEMINI / 22.7 CANCER
1975 LEO / 10.7 VIRGO
1976 CANCER / 15.7 LEO
1977 TAURUS / 6.7 GEMINI
1978 LEO / 12.7 VIRGO
1979 GEMINI / 7.7 CANCER
1980 CANCER / 22.6 GEMINI
1981 CANCER / 30.6 LEO
1982 TAURUS / 26.6 GEMINI / 21.7 CANCER
1983 LEO / 10.7 VIRGO
1984 CANCER / 15.7 LEO
1985 TAURUS / 6.7 GEMINI
1986 LEO / 12.7 VIRGO
1987 GEMINI / 6.7 CANCER
1988 CANCER / 22.6 GEMINI
1989 CANCER / 29.6 LEO
1990 TAURUS / 25.6 GEMINI / 20.7 CANCER
1991 LEO / 11.7 VIRGO
1992 CANCER / 14.7 LEO
1993 TAURUS / 5.7 GEMINI
1994 LEO / 11.7 VIRGO
1995 GEMINI / 5.7 CANCER
1996 CANCER / 22.6 GEMINI
1997 CANCER / 29.6 LEO
1998 TAURUS / 25.6 GEMINI / 20.7 CANCER
1999 LEO / 11.7 VIRGO
2000 CANCER / 14.7 LEO
2001 TAURUS / 5.7 GEMINI
2002 LEO / 11.7 VIRGO
2003 GEMINI / 5.7 CANCER
2004 CANCER / 22.6 GEMINI
2005 CANCER / 29.6 LEO
2006 TAURUS / 25.6 GEMINI / 20.7 CANCER
2007 LEO / 11.7 VIRGO
2008 CANCER / 14.7 LEO

VENUS THROUGH THE ZODIAC SIGNS

Venus in Aries

Amongst other things, the position of Venus in Aries indicates a fondness for travel, music and all creative pursuits. Your nature tends to be affectionate and you would try not to create confusion or difficulty for others if it could be avoided. Many people with this planetary position have a great love of the theatre, and mental stimulation is of the greatest importance. Early romantic attachments are common with Venus in Aries, so it is very important to establish a genuine sense of romantic continuity. Early marriage is not recommended, especially if it is based on sympathy. You may give your heart a little too readily on occasions.

Venus in Taurus

You are capable of very deep feelings and your emotions tend to last for a very long time. This makes you a trusting partner and lover, whose constancy is second to none. In life you are precise and careful and always try to do things the right way. Although this means an ordered life, which you are comfortable with, it can also lead you to be rather too fussy for your own good. Despite your pleasant nature, you are very fixed in your opinions and quite able to speak your mind. Others are attracted to you and historical astrologers always quoted this position of Venus as being very fortunate in terms of marriage. However, if you find yourself involved in a failed relationship, it could take you a long time to trust again.

Venus in Gemini

As with all associations related to Gemini, you tend to be quite versatile, anxious for change and intelligent in your dealings with the world at large. You may gain money from more than one source but you are equally good at spending it. There is an inference here that you are a good communicator, via either the written or the spoken word, and you love to be in the company of interesting people. Always on the look-out for culture, you may also be very fond of music, and love to indulge the curious and cultured side of your nature. In romance you tend to have more than one relationship and could find yourself associated with someone who has previously been a friend or even a distant relative.

Venus in Cancer

You often stay close to home because you are very fond of fami
and enjoy many of your most treasured moments when you are wit
those you love. Being naturally sympathetic, you will always d
anything you can to support those around you, even people yc
hardly know at all. This charitable side of your nature is your mo
noticeable trait and is one of the reasons why others are naturally s
fond of you. Being receptive and in some cases even psychic, yc
can see through to the soul of most of those with whom you con
into contact. You may not commence too many romant
attachments but when you do give your heart, it tends to l
unconditionally.

Venus in Leo

It must become quickly obvious to almost anyone you meet th
you are kind, sympathetic and yet determined enough to stand u
for anyone or anything that is truly important to you. Bright an
sunny, you warm the world with your natural enthusiasm and wou
rarely do anything to hurt those around you, or at least n
intentionally. In romance you are ardent and sincere, though son
may find your style just a little overpowering. Gains come throug
your contacts with other people and this could be especially tru
with regard to romance, for love and money often come hand i
hand for those who were born with Venus in Leo. People claim t
understand you, though you are more complex than you seem.

Venus in Virgo

Your nature could well be fairly quiet no matter what your Sun sig
might be, though this fact often manifests itself as an inner pea
and would not prevent you from being basically sociable. Son
delays and even the odd disappointment in love cannot be ruled o
with this planetary position, though it's a fact that you will usual
find the happiness you look for in the end. Catapulting yourself in
romantic entanglements that you know to be rather ill-advised
not sensible, and it would be better to wait before you committe
yourself exclusively to any one person. It is the essence of yo
nature to serve the world at large and through doing so it is possib
that you will attract money at some stage in your life.

Venus in Libra

Venus is very comfortable in Libra and bestows upon those people who have this planetary position a particular sort of kindness that is easy to recognise. This is a very good position for all sorts of friendships and also for romantic attachments that usually bring much joy into your life. Few individuals with Venus in Libra would avoid marriage and since you are capable of great depths of love, it is likely that you will find a contented personal life. You like to mix with people of integrity and intelligence but don't take kindly to scruffy surroundings or work that means getting your hands too dirty. Careful speculation, good business dealings and money through marriage all seem fairly likely.

Venus in Scorpio

You are quite open and tend to spend money quite freely, even on those occasions when you don't have very much. Although your intentions are always good, there are times when you get yourself in to the odd scrape and this can be particularly true when it comes to romance, which you may come to late or from a rather unexpected direction. Certainly you have the power to be happy and to make others contented on the way, but you find the odd stumbling block on your journey through life and it could seem that you have to work harder than those around you. As a result of this, you gain a much deeper understanding of the true value of personal happiness than many people ever do, and are likely to achieve true contentment in the end.

Venus in Sagittarius

You are lighthearted, cheerful and always able to see the funny side of any situation. These facts enhance your popularity, which is especially high with members of the opposite sex. You should never have to look too far to find romantic interest in your life, though it is just possible that you might be too willing to commit yourself before you are certain that the person in question is right for you. Part of the problem here extends to other areas of life too. The fact is that you like variety in everything and so can tire of situations that fail to offer it. All the same, if you choose wisely and learn to understand your restless side, then great happiness can be yours.

Venus in Capricorn

The most notable trait that comes from Venus in this position is that it makes you trustworthy and able to take on all sorts of responsibilities in life. People are instinctively fond of you and love you all the more because you are always ready to help those who are in any form of need. Social and business popularity can be yours and there is a magnetic quality to your nature that is particularly attractive in a romantic sense. Anyone who wants a partner for a lover, a spouse and a good friend too would almost certainly look in your direction. Constancy is the hallmark of your nature and unfaithfulness would go right against the grain. You might sometimes be a little too trusting.

Venus in Aquarius

This location of Venus offers a fondness for travel and a desire to try out something new at every possible opportunity. You are extremely easy to get along with and tend to have many friends from varied backgrounds, classes and inclinations. You like to live a distinct sort of life and gain a great deal from moving about, both in a career sense and with regard to your home. It is not out of the question that you could form a romantic attachment to someone who comes from far away or be attracted to a person of a distinctly artistic and original nature. What you cannot stand is jealousy, for you have friends of both sexes and would want to keep things that way.

Venus in Pisces

The first thing people tend to notice about you is your wonderful warm smile. Being very charitable by nature you will do anything to help others, even if you don't know them well. Much of your life may be spent sorting out situations for other people, but it is very important to feel that you are living for yourself too. In the main you remain cheerful, and tend to be quite attractive to members of the opposite sex. Where romantic attachments are concerned, you could be drawn to people who are significantly older or younger than yourself or to someone with a unique career or point of view. It might be best for you to avoid marrying whilst you are still very young.

CANCER:
2007 DIARY PAGES

October
2007

1 MONDAY
Moon Age Day 19   Moon Sign Gemin

You seem to be able to take life pretty much in your stride at th beginning of this new week and new month. October will offer yo significant incentives and you could do worse that to make a star by deciding what it is you want most from life. Concentrated effor definitely works best in the day ahead.

2 TUESDAY
Moon Age Day 20   Moon Sign Gemin

It pays to be up-front in all your dealings with the world at large Don't have secrets and be as open as you can with everyone. Th more others are instinctively aware that you are as pure as the drive snow, the greater should be the trust they have in you. Be carefu that you don't buy a pig in a poke if you are out shopping.

3 WEDNESDAY
Moon Age Day 21   Moon Sign Cance

The Moon returns to your zodiac sign and since it is also you ruling planet, that's got to be good news. Take all your vitalit today and aim it towards a dream that has been in your mind fo quite some time. Even the impossible is not beyond the bounds c credibility and at the very least you could achieve a grea compromise.

4 THURSDAY
Moon Age Day 22   Moon Sign Cance

You continue to be able to show a very positive face to the world a large. If you are seeking freedom, this is the time to make you pitch. In a physical sense you have scope to be energetic and to tak hurdles that would usually hold you back. Most important of all i the truly magnetic and attractive personality you can display.

50

5 FRIDAY
Moon Age Day 23   Moon Sign Leo

Someone, somewhere could be making you feel good with the attention they are heaping upon you. This might cause you to be slightly suspicious and although it is sensible to be on your guard, you might be going over the top. Why not accept that many people think you are great?

6 SATURDAY
Moon Age Day 24   Moon Sign Leo

If specific demands are being made of you at the moment, you might decide to spend some time sorting these out before you please yourself. It would be easy to get irritable with those you see as failing before they even try and you might even decide that in some cases it would be easier simply to do things yourself.

7 SUNDAY
Moon Age Day 25   Moon Sign Leo

Exciting times are possible ahead and it is worth taking a very close look at your finances in order to know whether you are in a position to spoil yourself in some way. Don't argue for your limitations or you will come face to face with them. It is better now to remain optimistic and to push forward in any way you can.

8 MONDAY
Moon Age Day 26   Moon Sign Virgo

Communication issues are highlighted at the moment and you could learn something that is to your definite advantage. This is a time to be in the know in a number of different ways, both for your own sake and with regard to your chief concern, which is always your family.

9 TUESDAY
Moon Age Day 27   Moon Sign Virgo

Things look good on the career front and especially so for those of you who have recently started a new job or else swapped responsibilities in some way. In addition to work you have a personal life too, and you shouldn't forget about it under present trends. Finding the right compliments to really knock someone off their feet could work wonders.

10 WEDNESDAY · *Moon Age Day 28 · Moon Sign Libra*

Hearth and home are important at the moment, but you may find your mind and your life somewhat split if a part of you also wants to be out and about. It ought to be possible to reach some sort of compromise with yourself and to share your time. Beware of getting tied down with petty rules and regulations today.

11 THURSDAY · *Moon Age Day 0 · Moon Sign Libra*

Trends assist you to turn your mind outward, away from the insular concerns that sometimes captivate you and towards the excitement that lies beyond your own front door. Despite the late date this would be an excellent time to take a break, and an impromptu holiday arranged around now could be good.

12 FRIDAY ☿ *Moon Age Day 1 · Moon Sign Libra*

The level of success you have at work today is specifically tied to who you know and the way you use the contacts you already have. Not that you need to focus your mind exclusively in the direction of your career. New social interests are there for the taking, probably ones to which friends introduce you.

13 SATURDAY ☿ *Moon Age Day 2 · Moon Sign Scorpio*

At this time social matters and group-based activities could well be attracting your attention. You might be quite keen to try something new and can easily enlist the support of your partner or maybe a good friend if you don't want to go it alone. There may be moments today when you will need to explain yourself.

14 SUNDAY ☿ *Moon Age Day 3 · Moon Sign Scorpio*

Time spent with friends today is certainly not wasted. If you display the warm and caring side of your nature, people should love to have you around. Attitude is very important if you are facing a change to your plans and have to adapt quickly. Self-belief isn't always present for the Crab, but you can make sure it is now.

15 MONDAY ☿ *Moon Age Day 4   Moon Sign Sagittarius*

There is a strong pioneering quality about you today, mainly encouraged by the position and aspects of the Moon in your solar chart. Rather than allowing yourself to be bulldozed into taking directions that are not of your own choosing, why not show that even easy-going Cancer can be stubborn on occasions?

16 TUESDAY ☿ *Moon Age Day 5   Moon Sign Sagittarius*

There are signs that any journey you undertake today could be fortunate and even exciting. It doesn't really matter whether you are moving about in connection with work or simply for social reasons – the change should do you good. Look out for personalities who enter your life around this time and make the most of their presence.

17 WEDNESDAY ☿ *Moon Age Day 6   Moon Sign Sagittarius*

The way to success in terms of personal relationships means keeping your feet on the ground and adopting a realistic attitude towards events. This may not prove to be the best romantic interlude of the month, but if it isn't, you can reassure yourself that this is through no fault of yours. The behaviour of others has a part to play.

18 THURSDAY ☿ *Moon Age Day 7   Moon Sign Capricorn*

You can afford to take life at a slower pace today and to allow others to make some of the running. If you have been in a position to offer another person some sort of training, it would now be sensible to see how well they can do. The lunar low might deter you from pushing ahead in a personal sense.

19 FRIDAY ☿ *Moon Age Day 8   Moon Sign Capricorn*

This is not a time during which you should be loading yourself down with too many burdens. The more you keep life light and airy, the less you should feel hampered by situations. The Crab is usually a big reader, and there won't be a better time this month to bury your head in a favourite book.

20 SATURDAY ☿ *Moon Age Day 9   Moon Sign Aquarius*

The lunar low passes away and you can return to a more progressive frame of mind. Specific decisions made today, even if they don't appear too important at the time, could be extremely significant in the longer-term. For this reason you would be wise to concentrate and to avoid making mistakes.

21 SUNDAY ☿ *Moon Age Day 10   Moon Sign Aquarius*

If you really want to have a pleasant day today it would be sensible to forget all about responsibilities and to enjoy yourself. This can be achieved best in the company of people you find relaxing to be with. Don't try to achieve anything important – simply settle down and appreciate the ride!

22 MONDAY ☿   *Moon Age Day 11   Moon Sign Pisces*

Your popularity could be at an all-time high, and that may prove to be especially useful to you. The people with whom you mix on a daily basis seem to have your best interests at heart and you can get them to move mountains to help you. It is at times such as this that you realise just how much you are appreciated.

23 TUESDAY ☿   *Moon Age Day 12   Moon Sign Pisces*

A period of harmonious relationships is on offer and should continue throughout most of today. You can use it to make sure that friendships are secure and happy and that you are feeling generally content with your lot in life. The only slight fly in the ointment could be that you are in some ways too comfortable.

24 WEDNESDAY ☿   *Moon Age Day 13   Moon Sign Pisces*

If you make instant decisions today you could live to regret the fact. A slower and steadier approach to most situations would now help, and even though you will occasionally be certain that you are right, you need to question your thinking. With just a little care, you can ensure things work out fine.

25 THURSDAY ☿ *Moon Age Day 14 Moon Sign Aries*

The time has now come to adopt a higher profile. If you've had a few days during which you have been fairly quiet and willing to take on board what others think, now is a time for positive action. Don't be surprised today if you attract romantic attention of some sort.

26 FRIDAY ☿ *Moon Age Day 15 Moon Sign Aries*

You can afford to feel more independent and enthusiastic – a far cry from the Crab who is sometimes on display. Although you still show great sensitivity of nature, you should now be more willing to overturn previous prejudices and to do what seems right to you. Not everyone will agree, but that's life!

27 SATURDAY ☿ *Moon Age Day 16 Moon Sign Taurus*

There is scope for you to focus on the material side of life during this weekend. If there is something you have been meaning to buy for your home, this could be as good a time as any to search it out. From a social point of view you might decide to stick to your inner circle around now.

28 SUNDAY ☿ *Moon Age Day 17 Moon Sign Taurus*

There are signs that relationships may not be working out quite the way you had intended. If those you care about the most are determined to be difficult, there might be very little you can do about the situation. It's worth showing your usual understanding, because your patience is sure to win out in the end.

29 MONDAY ☿ *Moon Age Day 18 Moon Sign Gemini*

Instant decisions are possible but not too potentially fortunate whilst the Moon occupies your solar twelfth house. In some way your mind could be confused, because a part of you is determined to push forward, whilst other components of your nature are telling you to wait in the shadows until you are more certain of yourself.

30 TUESDAY ☿ *Moon Age Day 19   Moon Sign Gemini*

It's possible to remain steady in your thinking and actions, but this state of affairs will not last beyond today. If you have time on your hands, it might be sensible to clear the decks for the actions that come along during Wednesday and Thursday. In personal attachments you need to avoid being too pushy.

31 WEDNESDAY ☿ *Moon Age Day 20   Moon Sign Cancer*

You can afford to feel very independent and enthusiastic today – just the right state of affairs to put your foot on the gas pedal of life and to make good headway. If you are certain in your thinking and your actions, you can make sure that no one gets in your way, and even usually awkward types will follow your lead without question.

November
2007

1 THURSDAY ☿   *Moon Age Day 21 Moon Sign Cancer*

The positive trends continue whilst the Moon occupies the zodiac sign of Cancer, and this is a period during which you can make even unexpected progress. Although you may sometimes be reticent to get rid of baggage that has accumulated in your life, now is a time when you should be much more willing to commit yourself to the future.

2 FRIDAY ☿   *Moon Age Day 22 Moon Sign Leo*

It is towards possessions and the way you view them that your mind is now encouraged to turn. You are entering a period during which 'things' will be far less important. It is for this reason that clearing out your cupboards and drawers can work wonders. For once the Crab could be deciding that it's best to travel light.

3 SATURDAY   *Moon Age Day 23 Moon Sign Leo*

Getting others to follow your line of reasoning ought to be quite easy today, not least because your powers of communication are to the fore. Finding the right words should be child's play, even though you might sometimes wonder at your own ingenuity. This is no time to maintain a sense of proportion!

4 SUNDAY   *Moon Age Day 24 Moon Sign Virgo*

Getting ahead of the game shouldn't be difficult. It is on days such as this that you have scope to realise your own intelligence and to use it to your advantage. Of course you can help others on the way, but there are some people around who seem determined to stick fast.

5 MONDAY
Moon Age Day 25   Moon Sign Virgo

Where tasks have to be dealt with today, the signs are that you want to do things your own way. You might even be a little cranky if things don't go as you wish and others will have to be careful not to step on your toes. What you can be quite sure of is your present ability to get most jobs done right first time.

6 TUESDAY
Moon Age Day 26   Moon Sign Libra

Your intuition can be stimulated today by any number of situations and you instinctively know when something looks or feels right. Don't be too quick to take offence with those who are genuinely doing their best, and try to be as fair with the world as the Crab usually is.

7 WEDNESDAY
Moon Age Day 27   Moon Sign Libra

The present position of Mercury in your solar chart assists in all matters to do with communication. Where you have had difficulty getting your message across you can now find ways and means to explain yourself. This has potential to be a better day in terms of personal attachments and romance in particular.

8 THURSDAY
Moon Age Day 28   Moon Sign Libra

It looks as though the Crab can be something of an explorer now and it is clear that you want to know what makes matters tick. This might not be the best part of the year to take a journey, but any opportunity you have to break the bounds of the normal and to see new places should be grabbed with both hands.

9 FRIDAY
Moon Age Day 0   Moon Sign Scorpio

It is your social life that has the most to offer right now, and trends help you to get in just the right frame of mind to start something new, possibly with a group or in some way associated with your locality. Routines are best dealt with early in the day, leaving you more time later in which to please yourself.

10 SATURDAY *Moon Age Day 1   Moon Sign Scorpio*

If you have to approach others today in order to gain the assistance you need to do things that seem important, don't forget to be grateful and to show the fact. The Crab can be just slightly offhand right now, and that could lead to a little resentment. You should have the confidence to broach a difficult subject.

11 SUNDAY *Moon Age Day 2   Moon Sign Sagittarius*

Twosomes are well highlighted under present trends and this would be the best part of the week to cement relationships that are important to you. For once Cancer may not want to go it alone, and even if you are still quite happy with your own company, in the main you are probably happier to have others on board.

12 MONDAY *Moon Age Day 3   Moon Sign Sagittarius*

Friendships can be great fun at the beginning of this new working week and you have every opportunity to turn colleagues into pals. Trends show new people entering your life a good deal around now, and you have scope to make sure that at least one person becomes someone who will be important to you for years to come.

13 TUESDAY *Moon Age Day 4   Moon Sign Sagittarius*

You can afford to enjoy helping others today and to go to great lengths to please those around you – even people you don't know too well. This might be a good time during which to ask for a few favours, and Tuesday should also be ideal for gradually breaking down anything that has been a difficult situation.

14 WEDNESDAY *Moon Age Day 5   Moon Sign Capricorn*

With the lunar low coming along you shouldn't be afraid to slow the pace of life significantly. Your powers of discrimination may be more limited and it might also be easy to run out of energy. This is not an ideal day to embark on any new project that takes both stamina and self-belief.

15 THURSDAY   *Moon Age Day 6   Moon Sign Capricorn*

It appears that you have a very short fuse for the moment, and you would be wise to count to ten in your dealings with people who tend to annoy you at the best of times. If you can't rely on the world at large, why not fall back on your own resources? The Crab could now be much quieter than of late.

16 FRIDAY   *Moon Age Day 7   Moon Sign Aquarius*

You are now entering a more emotional period and a time during which you have a chance to talk about the deepest of issues. The inner workings of the Cancerian mind is a closed book, sometimes even to you, but trends now assist you to share these unexplored regions with someone else.

17 SATURDAY   *Moon Age Day 8   Moon Sign Aquarius*

Chances are that you will now be making use of the help you can gain from others and may be able to achieve a closeness with a particular individual that has eluded you in the past. This could be because they are quite vulnerable at present, whilst you can be more honest and direct than might sometimes be the case.

18 SUNDAY   *Moon Age Day 9   Moon Sign Aquarius*

Even if you are content with your own company for the next couple of days, this doesn't mean you have to be either miserable or particularly withdrawn. It's just that if there are things that need to be done, you should instinctively realise that matters can be sorted quicker if you go it alone.

19 MONDAY   *Moon Age Day 10   Moon Sign Pisces*

This is probably the best day of the month to choose to be with loved ones, and even if the everyday responsibilities of your life are still present, it is those intimate moments that count for the most. Don't worry if you still show a tendency to be reflective and quiet. You can make the most important people in your life understand.

20 TUESDAY
Moon Age Day 11   Moon Sign Pisces

Money might not be the most important factor in your life at present, but it does have its part to play, and it's worth being aware of this fact now. Both medium- and long-term plans for increasing your wealth are favoured, and you should be quite happy to look at new and potentially lucrative possibilities.

21 WEDNESDAY
Moon Age Day 12   Moon Sign Aries

You may well prefer time spent away from emotional demands today and can afford to show a light and airy approach to life generally. There may not be time for too much reflection in any case and the thought of having to untangle the personal mess someone else is in probably won't be too appealing.

22 THURSDAY
Moon Age Day 13   Moon Sign Aries

Bear in mind that you can't trust every person you meet today and will need to be on your guard if you are not to be duped in some way. Rely on your instincts and don't overrule these with what seems like common sense. There is a little voice inside you that offers the very best advice and you would be wise to listen to it now.

23 FRIDAY
Moon Age Day 14   Moon Sign Taurus

What a good day this would be for discussions and debates. Your wit is potentially razor-sharp and you will be able to make just about anyone laugh, which is halfway to gaining your objective. You could even be somewhat calculating in your approach at the moment, but if everyone wins in the end, does it matter?

24 SATURDAY
Moon Age Day 15   Moon Sign Taurus

From being self-protective and thinking much more than usual about your own interests, you are now suddenly prompted to drop back into the more normal way of thinking for the Crab. This means being happy to exploit much of your energy in loving and protecting the people who are most important to you, both family and friends.

25 SUNDAY
Moon Age Day 16   Moon Sign Gemini

This is a great time to be with the ones you care about the most, whether you are doing something practical or simply having fun. You should be able to find something to do that stimulates your intellect, whilst at the same time proving to quite educational. Trends assist you to forge new long-term interests now.

26 MONDAY
Moon Age Day 17   Moon Sign Gemini

This may be a good time to withdraw somewhat, not because you are miserable or out of sorts with yourself in any way, but simply because you now work best on your own. These periods of self imposed isolation are not at all unusual for you, and this one is inspired by the position of the Sun in your solar twelfth house.

27 TUESDAY
Moon Age Day 18   Moon Sign Cancer

You can now afford to put new plans into operation and to break down barriers that have existed in a specific area of your life for some time. You can be like an irrepressible battering ram and you needn't stop until you have achieved your objectives. This is the power of the lunar high.

28 WEDNESDAY
Moon Age Day 19   Moon Sign Cancer

Once again you can make great gains by putting new plans of action into operation right now. Don't wait to be asked because you could lose the power of the moment. Now is the time to ask for what you want and maybe to take it in any case if those around you refuse to listen.

29 THURSDAY
Moon Age Day 20   Moon Sign Leo

Even if you are still showing a great deal of determination and perseverance it may not be quite as easy today to forge the important connections you really want to make. Maybe others are less approachable, or it could simply be that you are picking on the wrong sort of people in the first place.

30 FRIDAY
Moon Age Day 21   Moon Sign Leo

A day to concentrate on a specific issue, and not get too carried away with the insignificant details of life that don't really count for anything. Friendships prove to be very important and new casual attachments are possible for some Crabs. Getting really close to someone could be a different matter, and might prove difficult.

December
2007

1 SATURDAY
Moon Age Day 22   Moon Sign Virg

You can now attract great generosity of spirit from others at th
start of December, perhaps in return for favours you have don
them in the past. Even if you are not actively looking for support,
is there all the same. Your mind is very questioning at present an
especially with regard to issues that have a bearing on your home o
locality.

2 SUNDAY
Moon Age Day 23   Moon Sign Virg

With a slight change of emphasis in terms of planetary influences
is now possible for you to confuse others with what you are bot
saying and doing. It's worth taking just a little time out to explai
yourself because this can make all the difference. If you wer
looking for a peaceful Sunday, you could be somewha
disappointed!

3 MONDAY
Moon Age Day 24   Moon Sign Virg

There are signs that others want to be generous to you at th
moment, and you would do well to accept any offers that are mad
What people are doing is trying to repay you for the man
kindnesses you have shown to them, and you can take this as proo
of the sort of person you are.

4 TUESDAY
Moon Age Day 25   Moon Sign Libr

Optimism should remain generally high under present trends an
you might decide this would be a good time to push your luck jus
a little. There are some real advantages to be had at work and at th
same time you can make the most of some slightly better financi
luck than has been the case recently.

5 WEDNESDAY
Moon Age Day 26   Moon Sign Libra

There is a tendency now towards greater intimacy, even with people who have been slightly distant in the past. Nevertheless you can remain generally adventurous and might even decide to try something that has seemed intimidating in the past. By this evening you could well be organising social events for later in the month.

6 THURSDAY
Moon Age Day 27   Moon Sign Scorpio

A day to look out for some good fortune in financial matters and to spread your money around a little if you sense this is the right way to proceed. As usual you need to rely heavily on your intuition, especially when it comes to assessing whether people who are only now entering your life are really trustworthy.

7 FRIDAY
Moon Age Day 28   Moon Sign Scorpio

You should have a good instinctive understanding of people's motivation today and will not be easily fooled by anyone who has the clear intention of pulling the wool over your eyes. What could really annoy you is jargon and red tape, because your penetrating mind wants to go straight to the heart of any matter.

8 SATURDAY
Moon Age Day 29   Moon Sign Scorpio

Trends suggest that personal matters may need a greater amount of thought than you have offered them so far this week, and the weekend doubtless offers you the opportunity to look at a number of issues in greater detail. This is not a day to rush your fences and you can afford to be more pensive than of late.

9 SUNDAY
Moon Age Day 0   Moon Sign Sagittarius

If you really want to get on today you will have to put in a good deal more effort than might sometimes be the case. On the other hand, you should probably ask yourself if this might not be an ideal day to relax a little and to enjoy the entertainment that is brought to life by the antics of family members and friends.

10 MONDAY   *Moon Age Day 1   Moon Sign Sagittariu*

A favourable time to turn your attention to the material world. Witl everything to play for at the start of a new working week you wil want to be up early and getting on with a number of different jobs This is just as well because some notable delays are possible b tomorrow.

11 TUESDAY   *Moon Age Day 2   Moon Sign Capricor*

The lunar low could well be a time of detachment and a two-da period during which you are not really connected to the world a large in the way you have been so far this month. Your best respons is to treat this as a period for rest and relaxation and be willing t allow your friends to take some of the necessary strain.

12 WEDNESDAY   *Moon Age Day 3   Moon Sign Capricor*

Group situations can prove to be especially rewarding, even if yo decide to take something of a back seat for the moment. Althoug you sometimes use the period of the lunar low in order to retrea into yourself, this may not be the case today. On the contrar trends encourage you to seek out some company.

13 THURSDAY   *Moon Age Day 4   Moon Sign Capricor*

Even if today starts quietly, by the time lunchtime arrives yo should be right back in the groove and anxious to make headwa again. Romance seems to be very important under present trend and it's worth spending at least part of today telling someone ju: how important they are to you.

14 FRIDAY   *Moon Age Day 5   Moon Sign Aquarii*

This may well turn out to be a day of hectic comings and going: Keeping up with the general flow of life might not be at all eas especially if the people around you seem to be doing everythin they can to confuse matters. Rather than causing you irritation o distress, this situation can be seen as quite funny.

15 SATURDAY *Moon Age Day 6   Moon Sign Aquarius*

Although your vitality could sag somewhat at times throughout today, in the main you should be keen to get on with life and anxious to show your most positive face to most situations. Keep abreast of local news and views and don't forget a particular job that has been hanging over you for most of the week.

16 SUNDAY *Moon Age Day 7   Moon Sign Pisces*

This may be the first real time during December that you have been able to give some time to thinking specifically about Christmas. Don't forget those all-important invitations, and make sure that family gatherings are adequately organised. If there is one sign that needs to have the festive season sorted, it's yours.

17 MONDAY *Moon Age Day 8   Moon Sign Pisces*

Your love life is definitely favoured under present planetary trends, and those Crabs who are between relationships can use the run-up to Christmas to provide the embryo of something new and special. At work you might find a few frustrations developing, but you have the ability to take these in your stride.

18 TUESDAY *Moon Age Day 9   Moon Sign Aries*

You now have the knack of making sure your desires turn out pretty much the way you wish, even if you sometimes have to take a rather tortuous path in order to get things done. There is much humour about at the moment, and you may well be in a more happy-go-lucky frame of mind than has been possible so far this month.

19 WEDNESDAY *Moon Age Day 10   Moon Sign Aries*

You ought to be able to take advantage of more fortunate financial trends that crop up around now, and might also be pleased to lend a hand in the slightly difficult situations that surround certain friends. Routines can be boring, which is why you might decide to ring the changes whenever possible.

20 THURSDAY
Moon Age Day 11   Moon Sign Tauru

If there is a little more money around than you expected, why no
hang onto it? With Christmas in view there is a danger you will b
blowing everything you have on presents, but this could prove t
be a mistake. Not least you may well have a chance to discover som
amazing bargains if you wait for just a day or two.

21 FRIDAY
Moon Age Day 12   Moon Sign Tauru

You can display your versatility at the moment and you can tackl
routine and usual jobs in very new ways. Although you have one ey
on the upcoming festivities, you should also be very committed t
the everyday requirements life has of you. There are some re:
advantages on offer in your personal life.

22 SATURDAY
Moon Age Day 13   Moon Sign Gemin

Simply being yourself is the best key to happiness at the prese
time, though with the Moon in your solar twelfth house you coul
be slightly quieter than of late and anxious to spend an hour or tw
entirely alone. Splitting your time between solitary interludes an
the needs of your family is the balancing act for today.

23 SUNDAY
Moon Age Day 14   Moon Sign Gemin

Even if you seem to be slightly below par when it comes t
communicating, in the main you can get on better today than yo
might have expected. Why not see if you can get others to help yo
out with jobs that are irritating or boring? You can afford t
respond positively to the little favours others afford you.

24 MONDAY
Moon Age Day 15   Moon Sign Cance

Christmas Eve brings the lunar high and helps you to make this on
of the most positive and happy Christmas periods you hav
experienced for some time. Get the difficult jobs out of the wa
early in the day and if possible save some time to get to the shop
Most people hate town on a Christmas Eve, but not you. Look o
for some bargains.

25 TUESDAY   *Moon Age Day 16   Moon Sign Cancer*

You have so much going for you at the moment that it might be difficult to know in which way to turn your attention. Not only do you have plenty of charm and humour to make everyone else happy on this Christmas Day, you should be able to achieve a level of contentment that even the Crab rarely experiences.

26 WEDNESDAY   *Moon Age Day 17   Moon Sign Leo*

You can make sure this is an exuberant period, when you don't have to work very hard in order to get what you want from life. There are some interesting personalities about and you could be making a new friend. Romance is well highlighted and today could be the best day of Christmas in some respects.

27 THURSDAY   *Moon Age Day 18   Moon Sign Leo*

A chance word in the right direction could see you well set in terms of plans for the New Year. Even if you are fully enjoying what the festive season has to offer, it's also worth keeping one eye firmly placed on the future. In every respect you can now keep more balls in the air than a juggler.

28 FRIDAY   *Moon Age Day 19   Moon Sign Leo*

There are signs that involvement with friends could prove to be more complicated and difficult today than has been the case at any stage during December. In all probability this has little or nothing to do with you personally, but may be down to the complications in the lives of others. Be prepared to offer your special advice.

29 SATURDAY   *Moon Age Day 20   Moon Sign Virgo*

This would be a really good time to discuss things with family members. Maybe you are thinking about holidays for next year, or else a major change at home that will come along in the spring. Don't confuse issues any more than is necessary, and perhaps find the time to look carefully at all those Christmas presents!

30 SUNDAY

Moon Age Day 21   Moon Sign Virg

There are definitely helpful elements about on the path to progres today, even if some of them are disguised rather well. You have wha it takes to play the detective at present and to find out how everything works. Stand by for some real surprises when it comes t the lives and thoughts of your friends.

31 MONDAY

Moon Age Day 22   Moon Sign Libr

There are a few actions around today that could prove to be rathe self-defeating. Maybe you should content yourself by going wit the flow, because no matter how hard you try it is unlikely that yo will make much practical headway. New Year's resolutions may we start before the day is over.

CANCER:
2008 DIARY PAGES

CANCER:
2008 IN BRIEF

This is a year during which you need to start as you mean to go o and you should not allow the negative ideas of others to have bearing on your own life. January and February offer all the incentiv you need to get ahead at work and you should be especially we motivated at this time. Money matters are variable but planning fc the short and medium-term is definitely to be recommended.

March and April should find you feeling more relaxed and able t settle into situations than at the beginning of the year. You know wha you want, especially from personal attachments, and romance ough to play an important part in your life. April could bring a period c intensive spring-cleaning to every area of your life.

As the summer beckons, so May and June could find you lookin; for new things to do and places to visit. The better weather shoul entice you out of doors because that is where you will feel you greatest joy at this time. You seem to be entering a fairly lucky strea and can probably afford to speculate a little more than usual. Ther are many personalities entering your life at this time.

The warmer the weather gets, the happier you seem to be and Jul could turn out to be the happiest month of the year for the Crab. Jul and August offer you the chance to travel and since all opportunitie to see new places please the Crab, you should be in your element Don't be too critical of others and be willing to accept a different poin of view – even if you don't act on it.

With September and October comes a need for greater domesti security and a tendency to stick closer to home. This does not mean a end to your progressive attitude or to your travels. It merely infers tha your nearest and dearest will be the most important aspect of your lif and that you might prove to be more timid than was the case earlier.

November and December offer you a feast of possibilities - though there will be occasions when having a good time might prove to be both tedious and tiring. You need to balance the requirement of the festive season with your own longing for some quiet and solitude. If you manage this balance, Christmas should prove to be happy and rewarding. End the year with a determination to pick up the baton of life and to run with it. The incentives for the New Yea look especially good but the planning that turns them to your advantage has to begin before December is over.

January
2008

1 TUESDAY
Moon Age Day 23   Moon Sign Libra

The beginning of the year brings a very co-operative phase as far as you are concerned, suggesting that you can't do enough for those you love as 2008 gets going. In addition to your generosity you can also make use of a great deal of common sense and can get something sorted out that has been an irritant for a while.

2 WEDNESDAY
Moon Age Day 24   Moon Sign Libra

You have what it takes to get ahead at this time, and if you are back at work today you could be scoring a few successes. Over the festive period you have had time to think and to get things straight in your mind. It's now time to put your ideas into practice, and to find people who can be persuaded to lend a willing hand.

3 THURSDAY
Moon Age Day 25   Moon Sign Scorpio

This would be an excellent period for looking at changes that need to be made in and around your home. True, this is very early in the year for a spring-clean, but you might as well start as you mean to go on. If unnecessary clutter is annoying you under present astrological trends, you can be ruthless in eradicating it.

4 FRIDAY
Moon Age Day 26   Moon Sign Scorpio

You can project a very sparkling personality around now, even if the deeper side of your nature is also working very strongly. It isn't the obvious that really captivates your imagination and grabs your attention at present, but rather the undertones of life. You seem to know automatically how others are thinking.

5 SATURDAY *Moon Age Day 27   Moon Sign Sagittarius*

You have potential to find plenty to captivate you and to make life seem intriguing to say the least. Routines are easy to deal with if you embark on them with a song in your heart and a positive attitude. The same probably cannot be said to be the case for colleagues or relatives, some of whom may be really down at present.

6 SUNDAY *Moon Age Day 28   Moon Sign Sagittarius*

Don't be afraid to get into something new today and enjoy the possibilities that life is throwing in your path. You may show yourself to be somewhat more competitive now, and won't take kindly to losing in any sort of contest. You seem to be especially well suited to team sports or endeavours that offer you scope to co-operate with others.

7 MONDAY *Moon Age Day 29   Moon Sign Sagittarius*

There may be some radical alterations possible now, and old modes of thinking could be out of the window. Make good use of today because after this, trends encourage a much quieter and less progressive frame of mind until Thursday. Friends could prove to be especially useful when it comes to achieving a longed-for objective.

8 TUESDAY *Moon Age Day 0   Moon Sign Capricorn*

Today the Moon moves into your opposite zodiac sign of Capricorn, bringing that part of the month known as the lunar low. You may be less energetic at this time and more inclined to find a small corner in which you can sit and think. For Cancer this is no bad thing, because it is out of your musing now that success comes later.

9 WEDNESDAY *Moon Age Day 1   Moon Sign Capricorn*

Getting involved in interesting new projects may have to wait, because if you try too hard at the moment you could find yourself falling at the first hurdle. Why not let others take some of the strain whilst you cosset yourself a little? By tomorrow you can get back on fine form, but for the moment you will simply have to show some patience.

0 THURSDAY
Moon Age Day 2   Moon Sign Aquarius

ntense relationships seem to dominate your life and thinking today
ut you also need to show a light touch on occasions, and especially
 in your work. Even if family members are rather demanding, it is
iteresting to note how well you take such matters in your stride.
inancial success is within your reach as the days pass.

1 FRIDAY
Moon Age Day 3   Moon Sign Aquarius

leasant and unexpected happenings, in the main relating to your
iends, seem to dominate your life at the moment and many Cancer
ibjects may decide that the weekend is beginning early. Although
ou can still commit yourself positively to work, in the main you
ow have scope to seek more in the way of personal enjoyment.

2 SATURDAY
Moon Age Day 4   Moon Sign Pisces

rends assist you to get things to go your way in most respects this
eekend, and to actively seek ways to get ahead, especially in your
ome life. There are positive ways to show people how much you
re and these are not lost on you at the moment. Much of your
ind may still be focused on practical and financial matters.

3 SUNDAY
Moon Age Day 5   Moon Sign Pisces

 freedom-loving approach epitomises your attitude and actions on
is January Sunday. If you don't take kindly to being fettered in
iy way, your best approach is to seek any opportunity to ring the
anges. Most important of all is your need to travel, even if it is
ily as far as your local town. Variety is crucial.

4 MONDAY
Moon Age Day 6   Moon Sign Pisces

here can be a great deal to be gained today from discussions of
most any sort. Cancer can now afford to be chatty and confident,
 well as being anxious to let others know how your mind is
orking. Don't be too quick to jump to personal conclusions,
cause it is possible you are being deceived in some way. It's
iportant to be alert.

15 TUESDAY
Moon Age Day 7   Moon Sign Ari

A get-together of almost any sort could appeal to you now, an
particularly so if it allows you to get in touch with people yo
haven't seen for quite a while. It looks as though a good deal
your mind may be focused on the past today and tomorrow, but d
remember that the things that really matter lie in the future.

16 WEDNESDAY
Moon Age Day 8   Moon Sign Ari

The needs and wants of loved ones are inclined to prey on yo
mind today. There is nothing especially surprising about th
because it is the way you often think. However, it is also importar
to bear your own requirements in mind, because if you are nc
comfortable yourself you can't be of much use to anyone else.

17 THURSDAY
Moon Age Day 9   Moon Sign Taur

Mars is now in your solar twelfth house and as a result it might see
somewhat difficult to think big. However, the good thing abo
this planetary position is that it assists you to be deeply intuitiv
albeit in a very practical way. If you proceed by using your g
reactions you could find the successes beginning to arrive.

18 FRIDAY
Moon Age Day 10   Moon Sign Taur

You may decide that someone you haven't seen for ages shoul
make a return to your life, emphasising just how much the past
replaying for you at the moment. It's good to meet an old frien
particularly someone who was once so important to you. Howeve
you also need to remind yourself of the importance of today.

19 SATURDAY
Moon Age Day 11   Moon Sign Gemir

You can keep the weekend generally bright and cheerful, but t
fact that the Moon is now in your solar twelfth house does indica
a certain wistfulness that is likely to possess you from time to tim
This could make you more pensive than usual and incline you to b
especially attentive to your partner and family members.

20 SUNDAY   *Moon Age Day 12   Moon Sign Gemini*

If you remain serene but happy, you should be able to make much out of what is a generally cold and miserable time of year. You can find ways of warming things up, both for yourself and for those around you. Your imagination is also working strongly and will furnish you with ideas of how to entertain people who might be bored.

21 MONDAY   *Moon Age Day 13   Moon Sign Cancer*

The start of this new working week also encourages a change of attitude as far as you are concerned. The Moon has now moved into your own zodiac sign of Cancer, bringing that part of the month known as the lunar high. Keep your eyes open for Lady Luck, because you can make sure she comes into your life under such trends.

22 TUESDAY   *Moon Age Day 14   Moon Sign Cancer*

This is a time during which innovative changes count for a great deal. If you want to change your living or working environment, you should have everything you need to do so. Even if certain people seem to be throwing obstacles in your path, you can find ways and means to turn difficulties into genuine and long-lasting successes.

23 WEDNESDAY   *Moon Age Day 15   Moon Sign Leo*

It may be that you feel the need to assert yourself rather strongly, and if so you can take this as a legacy from the period of the lunar high. The only slight problem is if you don't have quite the same ability to bluff your way through situations as may have been the case yesterday. Perhaps just a little more caution is called for.

24 THURSDAY   *Moon Age Day 16   Moon Sign Leo*

There is a good deal of joy available now, and especially so with regard to your work. You can make even the most mundane chores fun and have scope to lift the spirits of colleagues and friends. Some special attention directed at your sweetheart or partner would not go amiss when the working day is over.

25 FRIDAY   *Moon Age Day 17   Moon Sign Virg*

Trends warn that an exciting plan of action could prove to b
something of a disappointment. If this turns out to be the case, you
best response is to retrench and begin again immediately. Only b
constantly applying yourself and by refusing to take no for a
answer can you really win through at the moment.

26 SATURDAY   *Moon Age Day 18   Moon Sign Virg*

You could now show a strong sense of adventure and can make th
most of this across much of the weekend. A day to be willing to p
yourself against almost any sort of challenge, and you can even sho
just how courageous the zodiac sign of Cancer can be. You
attitudes might slightly shock friends.

27 SUNDAY   *Moon Age Day 19   Moon Sign Libr.*

Your personality is now very impressive and you shouldn't have t
go far in order to create a good impression. Part of the result ma
be that you discover you have admirers you never even suspecte
For most this is a positive thing, but for one or two Cancerians it i
just possible that the fact could inspire a little jealousy.

28 MONDAY   *Moon Age Day 20   Moon Sign Libr.*

Life has potential to become hectic as the end of Januar
approaches, and it might occur to you that something you have ha
planned since before the start of the year is still waiting to be don
You are able to apply yourself to just about anything today, an
what is more it shouldn't bother you if you have to tackle severa
different tasks.

29 TUESDAY   ☿   *Moon Age Day 21   Moon Sign Libr.*

Whilst others mess around wondering how to do things in
theoretical sense, you pitch in and get them done. It is this ver
practical side of your nature that is going to be of most use to yo
today and which you can use to impress those around you. You ca
take certain situations by storm and it is at such times that you reall
begin to shine.

30 WEDNESDAY ☿ *Moon Age Day 22* *Moon Sign Scorpio*

The Crab is definitely on the move, and unlike that marine creature that is your namesake, you won't be scuttling anywhere sideways! On the contrary, you have what it takes to go straight for what you want and it is your very direct approach that is most likely to get you what you are seeking. You can positively shock people now!

31 THURSDAY ☿ *Moon Age Day 23* *Moon Sign Scorpio*

Any power struggles can be brought to a head now – simply because you are far less likely to back down in the face of opposition. Certain people may be about to discover just how powerful you can be, and you can make sure they are impressed. At home you show a different face and will be charm itself to those you love.

February
2008

1 FRIDAY
☿ *Moon Age Day 24*   *Moon Sign Sagittarius*

The first day of February offers a chance to take on new responsibilities willingly and to demonstrate just how well you deal with changing times. Some Crabs might even be considering a total change of career around this time, and if you are one of them, you can be fairly certain that you are doing the right thing.

2 SATURDAY
☿ *Moon Age Day 25*   *Moon Sign Sagittarius*

The start of the weekend allows you to carry on making a good impression, and the social side of your nature is well emphasised. No matter what the winter weather throws at you, there is scope for getting out of the house and doing something different. A shopping spree with friends might well appeal to you.

3 SUNDAY
☿ *Moon Age Day 26*   *Moon Sign Sagittarius*

Venus, now in your solar seventh house, turns out to be a fairly positive trend as far as you are concerned. It is supportive of existing love attachments and may also incline some Crabs to look again at a relationship that somehow fell by the wayside. Don't get bogged down by too many routines today, and remain essentially flexible.

4 MONDAY
☿ *Moon Age Day 27*   *Moon Sign Capricorn*

Relationships could be somewhat difficult to deal with today, but if so you can be fairly sure that it is not your attitude to blame. Your best response is to remain fair and wait until people calm down. This could be particularly true in the case of any work colleagues who are being anything but reasonable.

5 TUESDAY ☿ *Moon Age Day 28 Moon Sign Capricorn*

The lunar low offers a good time to take a break and to do something different. OK, so this is not an ideal time of year to go picnicking but there are many different sorts of outings and what you need most at the moment is the change. Try to do something that stimulates your intellect and which starts you thinking differently.

6 WEDNESDAY ☿ *Moon Age Day 0 Moon Sign Aquarius*

Anything new and unusual is inclined to captivate your imagination for the moment, and you can also be quite revolutionary in your thinking – well at least for a Cancer-born person. Your mind needs new stimulus, and you ought to be able to find people who have just what it takes to get you thinking in new directions.

7 THURSDAY ☿ *Moon Age Day 1 Moon Sign Aquarius*

Close emotional relationships could prove to be quite rewarding now, and it is towards these that you are inclined to look for your happiest moments. For some Cancer subjects there is the possibility that a new romance could be started at almost any time now, particularly if you are open to social opportunities.

8 FRIDAY ☿ *Moon Age Day 2 Moon Sign Aquarius*

Trends suggest that the smooth progress of your life can be somewhat affected by the unexpected behaviour of other people in your vicinity. You will have to take account of this, but in the main you should still be able to plough your own furrow. The attitude of family members especially could be quite puzzling on occasions today.

9 SATURDAY ☿ *Moon Age Day 3 Moon Sign Pisces*

Rather than giving in to either envy or jealousy today, why not show what a considerate and very giving sort of individual you are? Bear in mind that you may be being watched at the moment and some form of advancements might depend on the impression that you give. Be careful not to overspend right now.

10 SUNDAY ☿ *Moon Age Day 4   Moon Sign Pisces*

There could be new friendships on the horizon and at least some of these come about as a result of your present willingness to try new things. Spreading your wings is very important and you should not allow mundane issues to captivate you so much on this Sunday that you find little or no time to simply do what takes your fancy.

11 MONDAY ☿ *Moon Age Day 5   Moon Sign Aries*

It is towards the social side of your life that trends encourage you to turn at the beginning of this week. Even if you are working hard and achieving a good deal, nothing is really so important that you cannot take the odd hour out to do what you fancy. You might decide to persuade friends to join in.

12 TUESDAY ☿ *Moon Age Day 6   Moon Sign Aries*

This is one of the best times of the month for intimacy and for telling your partner how important they are to your life. You also presently have a good ability to mix business with pleasure, and can use this to be captivating and interesting to many different sorts of people. The Crab is magnetic now.

13 WEDNESDAY ☿ *Moon Age Day 7   Moon Sign Taurus*

A fairly mundane sort of day is a possibility as the Moon passes through your solar eleventh house, but you can use it to sort out a few details and also to get those around you working hard on your behalf. Don't give in to pessimism regarding monetary matters – simply find a different way to act.

14 THURSDAY ☿ *Moon Age Day 8   Moon Sign Taurus*

Mars remains in your solar twelfth house, assisting you to think very deeply about certain issues and encouraging you to keep anger bottled up. This really isn't good for you and it would be far better in most situations to say what you think. Like all Crabs, you know how to be diplomatic, so voice your opinions.

15 FRIDAY   ☿   *Moon Age Day 9   Moon Sign Gemini*

A couple of quieter days seem to be available, and you may not be breaking down the barriers of the possible today or tomorrow. What you can do is to make yourself more comfortable in some way, maybe by thinking about a series of small changes in and around your home. It's worth seeing what your partner thinks.

16 SATURDAY   ☿   *Moon Age Day 10   Moon Sign Gemini*

Today offers a chance to get on with small jobs and tasks that you know have to be done. Life might not be riveting, but you are the sort of person who can derive pleasure from the least expected directions. By the evening things could be starting to change significantly as the Moon races on towards your own zodiac sign.

17 SUNDAY   ☿   *Moon Age Day 11   Moon Sign Cancer*

You may now decide that the time is right for wholesale change and if there is any frustration about at all today, this comes because there is a limited amount you can do in a practical or a professional sense on a Sunday. Why not find ways to have fun, and at the same time drag others out of their lethargy?

18 MONDAY   ☿   *Moon Age Day 12   Moon Sign Cancer*

The lunar high continues to have a strong part to play in both your thinking and your actions. Even if you can't move mountains at the moment, you can tackle a few sizeable hills and the result will be greater satisfaction. Think of something you have wanted to do but in which you lacked courage and get on with it now.

19 TUESDAY   ☿   *Moon Age Day 13   Moon Sign Leo*

Your communication skills remain well accented, and you will be in an excellent position to get an idea across that has been floating around in your mind for some time. If the attitude of loved ones proves to be somewhat puzzling, you have what it takes to dig around until you are able to discover what is going on.

20 WEDNESDAY *Moon Age Day 14   Moon Sign Leo*

You can now deal very well with authority figures and need not be fazed by anyone, no matter how elevated they seem to be. You remain yourself in just about any company and can use your natural attitude and kind manner to impress people. An ideal day to spend some time with your partner or sweetheart and to speak your feelings.

21 THURSDAY *Moon Age Day 15   Moon Sign Leo*

Although there may be jobs around now that might seem to be nothing more than a chore, you can continue to plod away at them whilst others fall by the wayside. This is not without its own merits, because the fact that you won't give in will be noticed. There may be advancement on the horizon, so keep your ears open today.

22 FRIDAY *Moon Age Day 16   Moon Sign Virgo*

Optimism remains high and with Venus in your solar eighth house at the moment you have scope to make some sort of change with regard to your deepest attachments. For some this will mean a new romance, but for settled Crabs existing relationships can be given a definite spring-clean.

23 SATURDAY *Moon Age Day 17   Moon Sign Virgo*

If others make you feel good today, this is probably because of the sort of person you truly are. It is sometimes difficult for you to view yourself in the favourable light that others do and you should perhaps try a little harder to love the person you see in the mirror. However, your modesty can also be part of your immense attraction.

24 SUNDAY *Moon Age Day 18   Moon Sign Libra*

Compromises might not come especially easy today and particularly so if it seems that you are the one who is having to do all the giving. Trends now encourage you to dig your heels in and to refuse to move any further than a very definite point. That's fine if you make sure that those around you are willing to back off.

25 MONDAY
Moon Age Day 19   Moon Sign Libra

won't have escaped your attention that the year is moving on. March is on the horizon and the first flowers of spring are bedecking the hedgerows. This is usually a good time for you, and tends to feed your optimism during these dark winter days. Try to get some fresh air so that you don't miss the elemental quality of this period.

26 TUESDAY
Moon Age Day 20   Moon Sign Scorpio

If there is one thing that could get on your nerves at the moment it is if specific people swagger and brag all the time. There are ways and means to deal with these situations and you should be able to use your own methods to teach lessons. Your nature may be quieter than some, but you can still get your message across.

27 WEDNESDAY
Moon Age Day 21   Moon Sign Scorpio

A slight increase in self-confidence is possible, and it comes partially from the realisation that something you expected and planned for is now coming to fruition. You have what it takes to turn a few heads socially and should not allow yourself to be working all the time. A few domestic jobs could easily wait a while.

28 THURSDAY
Moon Age Day 22   Moon Sign Scorpio

An ideal time for someone you haven't seen for quite a while to make a return appearance in your life. This could well start you thinking again about the past – something the Crab is inclined to do a great deal. That's fine as far as it goes, but any real gains are firmly in the future and certainly not behind you.

29 FRIDAY
Moon Age Day 23   Moon Sign Sagittarius

Leap year day has potential to be quite eventful for you and could allow you to reach some important realisations regarding both work and your personal life. The attitude of a friend might be particularly surprising, and you can persuade others to take you on board when it comes to their own plans for the present and future.

March
2008

1 SATURDAY   Moon Age Day 24   Moon Sign Sagittarius

March brings with it a determination to do better in some way, though it's possible that you are being a little hard on yourself. Part of the problem today stems from the fact that the Moon is edging ever closer to your opposite zodiac sign of Capricorn, encouraging a tendency for you to be slightly more pessimistic.

2 SUNDAY   Moon Age Day 25   Moon Sign Capricorn

By all means get away from routines, but at the same time realise that this is not a day during which you can achieve a great deal in a practical sense. It might be better to leave one or two jobs on the shelf rather than to plough on knowing that you probably will not succeed in some way. Alternatively, you could decide to seek some assistance.

3 MONDAY   Moon Age Day 26   Moon Sign Capricorn

There could be a few financial ups and downs today, mainly influenced by the presence of the lunar low. It might be better to keep your purse or wallet shut for the moment, rather than risking losses that are not necessary. Colleagues could be somewhat difficult to get along with unless you show real patience.

4 TUESDAY   Moon Age Day 27   Moon Sign Capricorn

For the third day running the lunar low is around you, though it will be losing its power by the second part of today. You can afford to feel suddenly more optimistic and be able to deal with situations that might have got you down yesterday. The evening is a favourable time to push the boat out socially.

5 WEDNESDAY   *Moon Age Day 28   Moon Sign Aquarius*

At work and at home you have scope to feel quite comfortable and well able to take on situations that would have proved almost impossible at an earlier time. Be prepared to gather friends around you today and to make the most of your popularity. Getting to grips with a financial worry is also possible, and this should please you no end.

6 THURSDAY   *Moon Age Day 29   Moon Sign Aquarius*

There is a great deal of inspiration to be found today in the most surprising of places, which is exactly why you have to keep your ears and eyes wide open. Dealing in gossip can be diverting, and you may be happy to stop for a chat with almost anyone. Coming to grips with a domestic issue could require a whole new approach.

7 FRIDAY   *Moon Age Day 0   Moon Sign Pisces*

You can get a great deal from work situations at the end of this week, though Crabs who work at the weekend will continue to benefit from these trends across the next couple of days. By all means turn your attention to having fun once work is out of the way and get together with friends you might not see all the time.

8 SATURDAY   *Moon Age Day 1   Moon Sign Pisces*

General success is possible, though you may not be taking on very much in the way of challenges. It seems that a simple life suits you best for the moment and so at least some of your time can be spent getting rid of complications. In personal attachments you can show yourself to be quite sweet and very attentive.

9 SUNDAY   *Moon Age Day 2   Moon Sign Aries*

Look out for some light-hearted moments today because this is not a time during which you will want to take anything too seriously. Even if there are people around who seem determined to drag you into their difficulties and intrigues, your strength lies in refusing to become involved. The Crab can be very stubborn at times.

10 MONDAY   *Moon Age Day 3   Moon Sign Arie*

To get the very best from today you need to make certain that you are on the ball and that you keep up with what is happening around you. There is no time to slouch, and people will expect you to keep up, even if you are dealing with matters that are unfamiliar. It's hard, but the ground you can cover is amazing.

11 TUESDAY   *Moon Age Day 4   Moon Sign Tauru*

Trends stimulate a thirst for something new, and you may not be content with following the same old routines. At the same time you have scope to surround yourself with people who are very progressive and forward-looking so it should not be all that difficul to ring the changes in a number of different ways.

12 WEDNESDAY   *Moon Age Day 5   Moon Sign Tauru*

Your powers of persuasion are highlighted, and you can show yourself to be just as charming as the Crab is generally known to be. As a result this would be a good time to get something you want maybe not for yourself though, because you barely have a selfish bone in your body. You can get almost anyone to help you now.

13 THURSDAY   *Moon Age Day 6   Moon Sign Gemin*

A positive belief in your own abilities can be very important at the moment, though it has to be said that today and tomorrow may also be somewhat quieter than of late. Your confidence fizzes away silently, but people who are sensitive should recognise it all the same. Your reputation for being extremely capable could be growing.

14 FRIDAY   *Moon Age Day 7   Moon Sign Gemin*

From a practical point of view the Moon in your solar twelfth house will offer you something of a break from very demanding jobs, but underneath you are filled with determination. If friends seem especially interesting just now, you may decide to allow them to make the running – that is until tomorrow!

15 SATURDAY
Moon Age Day 8   Moon Sign Cancer

For the next three days the Moon occupies your own zodiac sign of Cancer, potentially offering one of the most positive and dynamic periods so far this year. Energy levels could well be off the scale and you can take the world by storm this weekend. What matters most now is having as much fun as possible.

16 SUNDAY
Moon Age Day 9   Moon Sign Cancer

The fact that this is a Sunday might make it difficult or impossible for you to address professional matters, so don't be afraid to use that energy in your social and personal life. You have a determination that is as big as a bus and it doesn't really matter in what direction you project it because success is there for the taking!

17 MONDAY
Moon Age Day 10   Moon Sign Cancer

This is a day for completing some projects and for getting others started. You can still fire on all cylinders and the only difference is that now you can put your energy to use in different ways. New partnerships could be formed at this time and it looks as though personal attachments are in for a very positive spell.

18 TUESDAY
Moon Age Day 11   Moon Sign Leo

You may be better focusing exclusively on professional duties and wishes for the moment, particularly if family and friends seem to be behaving in a rather untypical way. It looks as though you are well able to focus on practical matters and may stand a better chance of gaining the attention of those who are in charge.

19 WEDNESDAY
Moon Age Day 12   Moon Sign Leo

As often turns out to be the case in the end, you can now turn your mind back towards home and family. You care deeply for those with whom you live and may be spending a good deal of time at the moment doing what you can to make their lives more comfortable. In social situations trends support a slightly quieter approach.

20 THURSDAY
Moon Age Day 13   Moon Sign Virgo

For a number of different reasons you may well be especially busy at the moment. That's fine, just as long as you save at least an hour or two to concentrate on matters that please you exclusively. Some caution would be sensible with regard to speculation or business issues.

21 FRIDAY
Moon Age Day 14   Moon Sign Virgo

If you find yourself having to deal with authority figures today, your best approach is to be as open and honest as circumstances allow. Although the fact is sometimes lost on you, people love you just the way you are, so there is no point at all in trying to put on some sort of artificial front that the world likes less.

22 SATURDAY
Moon Age Day 15   Moon Sign Libra

The Crab could well feel the need to impress at the moment, and this comes from the present position of the Moon. You may also be proud of some recent achievement and can afford to let people know that your recent effort is bearing fruit. When it comes to the end of the day, the focus is on home-based matters.

23 SUNDAY
Moon Age Day 16   Moon Sign Libra

There are two opposing sides to your nature right now, each influenced by different planetary trends. On the one hand you feel a strong need to be around the people you know and love, whilst on the other you have a strong desire for fresh fields and pastures new. Stuck in the middle, it might be hard to decide what to do.

24 MONDAY
Moon Age Day 17   Moon Sign Libra

Progress is now possible in career matters, and many of the jobs that have to be done could seem like child's play to your more than capable nature. You might even decide to think up ways to complicate situations a little. Any thorny sort of problem is grist to the Crab's mill at the start of this week.

25 TUESDAY *Moon Age Day 18   Moon Sign Scorpio*

You continue to have what it takes to sort things out, and this could include the lives of your friends. If people come to you for advice, you won't be lacking when it comes to handing out that famous Cancerian common sense. All the same it might be advisable not to get too involved in the personal problems of others.

26 WEDNESDAY *Moon Age Day 19   Moon Sign Scorpio*

The Sun has now moved on into your solar tenth house and it brings with it a burning desire to do something different and, in particular, to travel. The year is marching on and there are sights to see that you have been promising yourself for several months. If time allows, why not take a few hours today to do something that is just for you?

27 THURSDAY *Moon Age Day 20   Moon Sign Sagittarius*

Strong romantic influences are about for you and it seems as though there might be something to prove as far as personal attachments are concerned. Try to do something to surprise your life partner and then stand back and watch the result. In a more practical sense, don't be afraid to tackle some financial planning.

28 FRIDAY *Moon Age Day 21   Moon Sign Sagittarius*

Life constantly offers new incentives to all of us – the trick lies in recognising them and in working out how best to use them to our advantage. At the moment you show yourself to be quite shrewd, and anyone who wanted to pull the wool over your eyes would have to be extremely astute. It's worth looking out for a genuine bargain today.

29 SATURDAY *Moon Age Day 22   Moon Sign Sagittarius*

You need change and diversity to start the weekend – not least because the lunar low is coming along tomorrow and that may well slow things down significantly. Today responds best if you are bold and enterprising, gaining ground and speed so that you can sail through the slightly more negative time ahead without realising that it is around.

30 SUNDAY   *Moon Age Day 23   Moon Sign Capricorn*

Trends encourage a quieter day, and there may be very little you can do about the situation. If you have gained sufficient momentum you should be able to pass over the lumps and bumps of life more or less unaware, though you may still be quieter than usual and more than happy to spend at least some time on your own.

31 MONDAY   *Moon Age Day 24   Moon Sign Capricorn*

This may not be a particularly positive or dynamic start to the week. In the main it might be best to allow those around you to make most of the running, whilst you sit on the riverbank of life and watch the water flow by. By tomorrow there will be a more interesting picture to look at, but for the moment your best approach is to be patient.

April
2008

1 TUESDAY
Moon Age Day 25   Moon Sign Aquarius

If you are an April Fool today it is only because you are allowing the situation to take place. Nobody could confuse or trick you when your mind is working as well as it is at the moment. All the same your sense of fun is well highlighted, and you have what it takes to join in all the jokes and even to instigate many of them.

2 WEDNESDAY
Moon Age Day 26   Moon Sign Aquarius

You have what it takes to work extremely well today when co-operating with others and in business partnerships. Some small distractions of a personal sort might get in the way, but the main emphasis for today is towards practical and professional matters. Even friendship can take a back seat for once.

3 THURSDAY
Moon Age Day 27   Moon Sign Pisces

There are many rewards about for the taking, but before you can gain them you need to be sure of yourself and your thinking. This is no time to doubt your own capabilities and neither should you listen to the ranting of people who don't know what they are talking about. A day to rely on the courage of your own convictions.

4 FRIDAY
Moon Age Day 28   Moon Sign Pisces

Now would be a great time to share things with both your colleagues and your friends. Even if family and domestic matters are taking a back seat, that shouldn't matter because you can catch up on that area of your life later. For now you can take advantage of greater power to rule your own professional life.

5 SATURDAY
Moon Age Day 29   Moon Sign Pisces

Even if a social contact on whom you were relying lets you down this weekend, in the end it shouldn't matter because you are so well able to think on your feet. Set out to have a good time today and get yourself out there into the midst of a busy and intriguing world. Fascination comes in all shapes, sizes and forms today.

6 SUNDAY
Moon Age Day 0   Moon Sign Aries

It might now become clear that a very careful handling of your finances is absolutely necessary. This fact should not be allowed to get in the way of you simply enjoying yourself – most likely in the company of people whose presence in your life is so important. Even normally difficult people can be persuaded to join in the fun.

7 MONDAY
Moon Age Day 1   Moon Sign Aries

The potential for attracting new individuals into your life now is very good indeed. It might seem at times as if you are so busy that you don't have the time to concentrate on anything as deeply as you would wish, but you do have what it takes to keep up. You can afford to leave alone routines that have the ability to drive you crazy.

8 TUESDAY
Moon Age Day 2   Moon Sign Taurus

It isn't simply that you have the ability to gather people around at present, but rather the sort of person you can attract. Almost anyone who comes new into your life right now has an important part to play in your present and future. Make the most of your intuition and your great knack for sizing up situations.

9 WEDNESDAY
Moon Age Day 3   Moon Sign Taurus

Not everyone seems to be equally helpful today, but maybe that is because your needs and theirs seem to work against each other. If you put your mind to the situation you can easily think up ways to please almost everyone, though there may still be someone who feels left out in the cold, and you can't alter that.

0 THURSDAY · Moon Age Day 4 · Moon Sign Gemini

ry not to rush things too much today because if you do there are
ely to be some bloomers made! The Crab works best when it can
ove steadily towards its chosen objectives and this is true even
here routine tasks are concerned. If you do go at jobs too fast you
ight have to do some of them again later.

1 FRIDAY · Moon Age Day 5 · Moon Sign Gemini

you avoid being in too much of a rush – this time with money –
u stand a chance of getting something you have been wanting for
while. There are bargains to be had at the moment but you will
ve to look carefully in order to find them. Meanwhile you can
ake this an interesting time as far as romance is concerned.

2 SATURDAY · Moon Age Day 6 · Moon Sign Cancer

e Moon moves into your zodiac sign at just the right time to
fer good incentives for the weekend. Although the lunar high
ight not be of much use to you in a professional sense this
eekend, it can offer you greater energy, together with a
termination to paint the town red in some way.

3 SUNDAY · Moon Age Day 7 · Moon Sign Cancer

mething you hear on the grapevine is worth following up on
day because you clearly have what it takes to dig away until you
t the answer you are looking for. If you get Lady Luck on your
de, a little limited speculation might be in order. In a social sense
u can make sure almost everyone finds you interesting and
ractive now.

4 MONDAY · Moon Age Day 8 · Moon Sign Leo

ose co-operation with others can bring its own rewards today,
ough trends encourage you to concentrate more on family and
mestic life than on professional or practical issues. It might be
nsible to hand out a few compliments when you can, because this
ll get you noticed more and elicit a positive response.

15 TUESDAY
Moon Age Day 9   Moon Sign L

You could be in for a slightly taxing time, but since you are n
usually frightened of a little hard work this should not be too mu
of a problem. Certain people could be awkward to deal with, ar
this might come as a surprise, particularly if it is individuals wh
rarely give you a problem. Simply lock into that Cancerian patienc

16 WEDNESDAY
Moon Age Day 10   Moon Sign Vir

It is just possible that your sense of personal freedom is bei
slightly stamped upon by family or domestic responsibilities. Wh
you need to do is to let someone else take the strain for a whil
leaving you able to do something different. Even a break of a fe
hours could help you to feel a whole lot better about life.

17 THURSDAY
Moon Age Day 11   Moon Sign Vir

It is within the realms of teamwork that you can gain your be
rewards right now. It's possible that all sorts of people look to yo
for guidance, and though you don't monitor the fact on a momer
by-moment basis, you are very important to the way things happe
Now you may be looked to for leadership.

18 FRIDAY
Moon Age Day 12   Moon Sign Lib

Even if in some ways it seems as though you are looking on th
negative side of life, you can do so in a very humorous way. Th
allows you to make other people laugh, which in turn ought
cheer you up no end. The Crab doesn't see itself as being a natu
comic, but is encouraged to be one under present trends.

19 SATURDAY
Moon Age Day 13   Moon Sign Lib

Whilst your current attempts to get ahead may seem fraught wi
small but significant problems, at the same time you can retain th
sense of humour and show a great willingness to do things as ma
times as proves to be possible. That sort of patience has potential
bring its own rewards and also makes it easy to find help.

0 SUNDAY · · · · · · · · · *Moon Age Day 14 · · Moon Sign Libra*

ou may need a slightly more frugal approach when it comes to
nances, particularly if there is slightly less money available now
an you might have expected or hoped. Here's the good news.
ost of what really takes your fancy on this spring Sunday needn't
ost you a penny.

1 MONDAY · · · · · · · · · *Moon Age Day 15 · · Moon Sign Scorpio*

ncharacteristically you might decide to retreat from challenges at
e start of a new working week, and if so you can blame the present
osition of the Moon for encouraging a timorous approach. All the
me it would be a shame because it appears that in some ways you
uld be closer than ever to achieving a longed-for objective.

2 TUESDAY · · · · · · · · · *Moon Age Day 16 · · Moon Sign Scorpio*

social boost is available. Venus in your solar tenth house can also
rove to be very useful when it comes to deeper, more personal
tachments. Crabs who are looking for new love have potential to
nd it now, and many of you may have social opportunities that
ome like a bolt from the blue. Don't hesitate today!

3 WEDNESDAY *Moon Age Day 17 · · Moon Sign Sagittarius*

/ith everything to play for, you can make this one of the most
teresting periods of the month. You show yourself to be keen to
ke up anything new and should be well able to concentrate. There
ay be distractions around, but most of these seem to be of a fairly
inor nature and may in themselves be fortunate.

4 THURSDAY *Moon Age Day 18 · · Moon Sign Sagittarius*

ven if you feel a degree of stress today you can come through it
ith all flags flying, and it is your natural kindness and sincerity that
ows through. This makes you particularly attractive to others. All
e attention you elicit should tell you something about your
opularity, but you can be quite blind on occasions.

25 FRIDAY   *Moon Age Day 19   Moon Sign Sagittari*

If professional progress slackens as the working week draws to
close, why not use the time to please yourself? The weekend ahea
is somewhat restricted because of the lunar low, which is why yo
should probably get anything important out of the way later toda
allowing time for reflection and relaxation later.

26 SATURDAY   *Moon Age Day 20   Moon Sign Capricor*

So much this weekend depends on your attitude and the approac
you take to life. If you accept from the start that you might n
achieve very much in a practical sense, you can abandon a few
your efforts for a while and instead can turn to having fun at
personal level. If you do so, the worst aspect of the lunar low
mitigated.

27 SUNDAY   *Moon Age Day 21   Moon Sign Capricor*

This will be another day during which you need to concentrate c
matters that have no practical value but which are important all tl
same. It's worth listening to family members and what they have
say. Buy a bunch of flowers or some other gift for your sweethear
fluff up your feathers and enjoy a comfortable Sunday!

28 MONDAY   *Moon Age Day 22   Moon Sign Aquari*

What a change you can make today! Both the Sun and the Moo
are poised to offer you something special at the beginning of th
week and you ought to be feeling pretty good about yourself an
your life. Of course you can't expect everything to go your way, b
you should be particularly good at changing direction if necessar

29 TUESDAY   *Moon Age Day 23   Moon Sign Aquari*

The Sun now occupies your solar eleventh house and that is positi
as far as you are concerned. You seem to have what it takes to see w
ahead of yourself and so the sort of decisions you are taking shou
have a great bearing on your life in the weeks and months ahea
Many Crabs might now be planning a journey that comes later.

30 WEDNESDAY   Moon Age Day 24   Moon Sign Aquarius

The most potent planetary influence around you at present is that of Mars in your solar first house. This offers a greater degree of certainty about your own life and an ability to say what you think to a greater extent. It's rare for the Crab to be anything other than charming and diplomatic, but your nature does have an edge now.

May

2008

1 THURSDAY
Moon Age Day 25   Moon Sign Pisces

It's the first day of May – a fact that is hardly likely to be lost on a summer-born sign like Cancer. Why not take some time out to see the flowers growing and to feel the growing warmth in the breeze? Even if you only find the time to walk in the park or along a lovely avenue, this little exercise will do you no end of good right now.

2 FRIDAY
Moon Age Day 26   Moon Sign Pisces

A degree of re-evaluation is now possible in terms of personal relationships. It isn't that you want to change them altogether, merely that you feel a little tinkering is in order. It could be that you feel as if someone is starting to take you for granted and as a result you might decide to do something to make them realise the fact.

3 SATURDAY
Moon Age Day 27   Moon Sign Aries

What matters most today is your ability to communicate. The weekend goes much better for you if you are out there in the big, wide world, and you probably won't achieve much if you are stuck at home. A day to be confident in your ability to make a good impression and to go for gold in all sporting and social activities.

4 SUNDAY
Moon Age Day 28   Moon Sign Aries

Even if you are taking nothing for granted today, there may be happenings that come as a real surprise. For example, you might hear from someone you haven't been in touch with for a very long time, or else could be somewhat taken aback by a communication from an individual who lives at a great distance.

5 MONDAY
Moon Age Day 0   Moon Sign Taurus

Don't be in too much of a hurry today. The planets indicate that if you are willing to take your time you can achieve a great deal more than you would by rushing. This is as true in personal matters as it is likely to be at work. Fortunately you are the sort of person who automatically appreciates the benefits of doing things properly.

6 TUESDAY
Moon Age Day 1   Moon Sign Taurus

The focus is on more responsibilities this week, and you might worry from time to time about this. Actually you are one of the most responsible people to be found anywhere in the zodiac and are far more capable than you believe yourself to be. Sometimes you have to be stretched a little in order to realise the fact.

7 WEDNESDAY
Moon Age Day 2   Moon Sign Gemini

Business dealings are well marked at the moment, and you can work especially well in partnerships. Cancerians who are self-employed could make the most progress of all and might well discover around now that they have a string to their bow that they never suspected before.

8 THURSDAY
Moon Age Day 3   Moon Sign Gemini

Relationships could throw up the odd difficulty at present and these come along at a time when you might rather be quiet and pensive. Instead of being able to curl up in a corner with a book you may have to work out why others are behaving in such a strange way. Fortunately, you can bring an element of comedy to the situation.

9 FRIDAY
Moon Age Day 4   Moon Sign Cancer

You have what it takes to be at the forefront of any action that is taking place in your vicinity and more than this, you might even be the one who is instigating a good deal of it. The lunar high supports a bright and breezy attitude, full of beans and anxious to make the most favourable impression possible. You may even shock a few people!

10 SATURDAY
Moon Age Day 5   Moon Sign Cancer

Getting one over on the competition should not be hard for the moment. Trends suggest that rules and regulations now mean little or nothing to you, and you make almost everyone gaze at you in utter surprise. It looks as though the Crab is really coming out of its shell and the result can be sizzling and sensational.

11 SUNDAY
Moon Age Day 6   Moon Sign Leo

Emotional matters could dominate in personal attachments and you might find it slightly more difficult than usual to tell your partner exactly how you are feeling about certain situations, particularly if you don't know yourself. A leave of absence from tricky issues could work wonders, so why not take some time out?

12 MONDAY
Moon Age Day 7   Moon Sign Leo

New and unusual ideas are available from all sorts of directions and it looks as though the Crab is just about as ingenious as it is possible to be. Not only can you be particularly inventive, you also have what it takes to turn some of your most flamboyant schemes into reality. Changes at home are also well indicated.

13 TUESDAY
Moon Age Day 8   Moon Sign Virgo

One of the problems occasionally encountered by Cancerian individuals is the tendency to look back and analyse the past. As a yardstick for future actions this might be useful, but in the main what matters is the present and future. This is worth remembering under present planetary trends so avoid too much nostalgia.

14 WEDNESDAY
Moon Age Day 9   Moon Sign Virgo

You can gain a great deal at the moment from simply knowing what is going on around you. For this reason, and also because it's just good on occasions, be prepared to join in with any gossip that is taking place around you. This can be within your home environment, but might also take place in social or working situations.

15 THURSDAY
Moon Age Day 10   Moon Sign Virgo

Communications are favoured, encouraging you to show your chatty side. There are strong indications at the moment that you can make hard, financial gains from travel, as well as being able to enjoy yourself on the way. As a result this is probably not the best time of the month to stand still or to lock yourself away.

16 FRIDAY
Moon Age Day 11   Moon Sign Libra

Even if you aren't especially motivated by material success as a rule, trends assist you to look towards any gains you can make at the moment. These are most likely to be of a financial nature and your usual shrewd approach is particularly well accented at this time. You should take advantage of some general luck.

17 SATURDAY
Moon Age Day 12   Moon Sign Libra

You may find loved ones difficult to assess this weekend, which is why the wisest Crabs could be spending as much time as possible with friends. Even your partner or sweetheart can be difficult to deal with, though they will be less of a problem when you are involved in group situations. Today might be especially good for shopping.

18 SUNDAY
Moon Age Day 13   Moon Sign Scorpio

Information is available now that could prove to be somewhat misleading. Fortunately the sign of Cancer makes for a very shrewd attitude, so it isn't very often that you are fooled. In particular, you would be wise to stay away from get-rich-quick schemes that seem a little too good to be true. Following your instincts is now vital.

19 MONDAY
Moon Age Day 14   Moon Sign Scorpio

There are signs that it may be necessary to delve into the past in order to solve a problem in the present. Although the advice generally this month has been to avoid looking back, there are exceptions, and today seems to be one of them. Analysing your actions some time ago can help you to avoid making the same mistake again.

20 TUESDAY *Moon Age Day 15   Moon Sign Scorpio*

In a general sense you can be on good form at the moment, and the only possible irritant comes from the direction of friends or associates, some of whom seem to be especially demanding. This is something you can take in your stride, though you may occasionally long to say 'get me out of here'!

21 WEDNESDAY *Moon Age Day 16   Moon Sign Sagittarius*

Even if not everyone appears to be on your side today, beware of making cast judgements because you could be wrong. Trends encourage a strong desire for change, and the more the year advances, the greater might be your yearning need to get away from routine situations. Any form of journey around this time would be no bad thing.

22 THURSDAY *Moon Age Day 17   Moon Sign Sagittarius*

Today has potential to be quite entertaining, even if you decide to make most of the running yourself. A couple of quieter days are on offer, so it is worth your while today putting in that extra bit of effort that can make all the difference. By the evening the lunar low begins to appear, so don't be afraid to take a rest.

23 FRIDAY *Moon Age Day 18   Moon Sign Capricorn*

Whilst some people find the lunar low extremely difficult to deal with, as a rule you don't. This is partly because the Moon is your ruling planet and so none of its positions are entirely bad for you, but also because you do have a distinctly quieter side to your nature that responds rather well to occasional periods of solitude.

24 SATURDAY *Moon Age Day 19   Moon Sign Capricorn*

Today responds best if you keep yourself to yourself, and the only problem that this raises is if relatives and friends think you might be sulking about something. It's pointless trying to convince them that you are fine, and in any case the Moon only stays in the zodiac sign of Capricorn until tomorrow.

25 SUNDAY   Moon Age Day 20   Moon Sign Capricorn

Even if today starts out uneventful and even a little dull, there is no reason why this should continue all day. On the contrary, by just after lunch the Moon moves into Aquarius, assisting you to come out of yourself. Romance is especially well highlighted today, so why not sweep someone off their feet?

26 MONDAY   Moon Age Day 21   Moon Sign Aquarius

This can be a great time to simply be you. The Crab is not generally the most outgoing or confident creature in the zodiac, but there are times during which you have what it takes to positively shine. The present position of the Sun and a plethora of other good planetary positions can help you to make this a very positive time.

27 TUESDAY   ☿ Moon Age Day 22   Moon Sign Aquarius

What you seek today – and what you have scope to find – is independence. You may not take at all kindly to being told what to do, and will be at your very best when people look towards you for instruction and guidance. This is partly why it's worth sticking to situations you understand well. Life continues to look good.

28 WEDNESDAY ☿   Moon Age Day 23   Moon Sign Pisces

An argumentative attitude on your part could lead to unnecessary difficulties, and because of your present independent stance it could well be you who is the chief protagonist. People could react strongly, and you need to find ways in which to defuse potentially difficult situations long before they get out of hand.

29 THURSDAY ☿   Moon Age Day 24   Moon Sign Pisces

Venus is in your solar twelfth house now, offering a chance to smoulder in an emotional sense. This is not at all a bad thing because you can be at your sexy, mysterious best. When it comes to attracting people you fancy, trends lend a helping hand, though your own power might astound you.

30 FRIDAY ☿ *Moon Age Day 25 Moon Sign Ari*

A day to put your personal strengths on display and to make gain simply by being yourself. You still have a little of the mysteriou about you and it might be sensible to feed this tendency in order t create an air of anticipation in the minds of admirers. From romantic point of view, you can make this a favourable time.

31 SATURDAY ☿ *Moon Age Day 26 Moon Sign Ari*

Even though you are presently as perceptive as it is possible for yo to be, there are still limits to your mental and persuasive powers You might decide today to rely on the good offices of other people whilst being absolutely scrupulous in your determination not t start arguments or even to take part in them.

June

2008

1 SUNDAY ☿ *Moon Age Day 27* *Moon Sign Taurus*

As is often the case, you may well go to great lengths today in order to please other people. There's nothing at all wrong with that but you can sometimes go too far. A little more in the way of a selfish attitude would not be a bad thing under present planetary trends. In any case, by making gains yourself you can help others along too.

2 MONDAY ☿ *Moon Age Day 28* *Moon Sign Taurus*

There are plenty of different options about today, so you needn't accept what you know to be second-best. Instead of just taking what people are offering, you can afford to push them to make greater concessions. This is especially true if you are out shopping because there are some real bargains to be had if you are willing to do a little haggling!

3 TUESDAY ☿ *Moon Age Day 29* *Moon Sign Gemini*

You can keep your love and social life on a definite roll at the moment. You can use your tendency to smoulder emotionally in order to attract would-be admirers, but you are also extremely funny at present, which is also attractive. Even the odd mistake you make right now can be turned to your advantage.

4 WEDNESDAY ☿ *Moon Age Day 0* *Moon Sign Gemini*

The time is right to let go of all prejudices and to enjoy yourself, especially when you are in good company. This need not be only when you are in social situations, because you can gain stimulation from colleagues and even casual acquaintances right now. Almost every situation has its strong points for the Crab at present.

5 THURSDAY ☿ *Moon Age Day 1   Moon Sign Cance*

This has potential to be the most positive and dynamic lunar high so far this year. This is because the position of the Moon in you sign of Cancer is well backed up by a whole host of other positiv planetary positions. Make the most of today by being willing t have a go at anything, and do all you can to attract others.

6 FRIDAY ☿ *Moon Age Day 2   Moon Sign Cance*

If you continue to act and think in a very positive way, you hav scope to get a very good reaction from others. Those people wh come into your life around this time could prove to be o tremendous use to you both now and in the near future, and yo can afford to emphasise and enjoy your social life in particular.

7 SATURDAY ☿ *Moon Age Day 3   Moon Sign Le*

Despite the fact that the Moon has moved on you can continue t show a very positive face to the world at large. You are still able t attract others, sometimes even when you don't mean to do so, an you might have just a little trouble getting rid of individuals who ar proving to be somewhat tiresome or irritating.

8 SUNDAY ☿ *Moon Age Day 4   Moon Sign Le*

It shouldn't take much in the way of effort for you to put yoursel in the midst of potentially exciting and very enjoyable situations a the moment. If anything, you might be having too much fun, and could decide by the end of the day that it would be just as much fun to slump down in your favourite chair and rest for a while!

9 MONDAY ☿ *Moon Age Day 5   Moon Sign Le*

Your strength lies in your great self-awareness and your ever-greater ability to express your views and to get your message across exactly as you would wish. Today is a period when gains can be made almost unexpectedly, and you can make sure you are flavour of the month with more than a few people.

10 TUESDAY ☿ *Moon Age Day 6* *Moon Sign Virgo*

There could be a few difficulties about today, perhaps inspired by people who seem determined to be awkward. Rather than wasting your time arguing with such individuals it would be far better simply to do your own thing and to ignore contrary advice. Socially speaking the day has its ups and downs but offers reasonable opportunities.

11 WEDNESDAY ☿ *Moon Age Day 7* *Moon Sign Virgo*

Be prepared to emphasise your separateness from the crowd by being as different as proves to be necessary. The Crab is often a quiet creature and very rarely sets out to rock any boat, but this needn't be the case at the moment. Why not put on your wildest outfit and let everyone know that the Crab is up for some fun?

12 THURSDAY ☿ *Moon Age Day 8* *Moon Sign Libra*

This is a very strange period for you, because although planets such as Mars and the Moon presently offer a boost, at the same time the Sun is in your solar twelfth house. This means there are two very distinct sides to your nature, and is also a sure indication that your powers of perception are to the fore.

13 FRIDAY ☿ *Moon Age Day 9* *Moon Sign Libra*

Even if you are on top form as far as communication issues are concerned, you should avoid getting involved in needless competitions with others, simply for the sake of the exercise. Don't be afraid to work towards your own objectives, whether or not the consensus is on your side. You can win out in the end.

14 SATURDAY ☿ *Moon Age Day 10* *Moon Sign Scorpio*

Looking at the different possibilities of life may well take up some of your time during the first part of the day, but in the main you can remain as positive as you have been for a few days. You can afford to take time out to enjoy yourself and to do what you can to lift the spirits of friends.

15 SUNDAY   ☿ *Moon Age Day 11   Moon Sign Scorpio*

In the short term it might be sensible to make a list of things that need to be done and to approach them in the order of their importance. However, it's worth focusing a part of your mind on the future, and it is just as important to have some time to sit somewhere quiet and contemplate your intended actions.

16 MONDAY   ☿ *Moon Age Day 12   Moon Sign Scorpio*

This would not be a particularly good day for hedging your bets or for putting your personal powers to the test. The influence you have over life may be slightly limited at the start of the day, but you can improve it later. You have scope to develop an idea that was born during the weekend, and this could become a major focus.

17 TUESDAY   ☿ *Moon Age Day 13   Moon Sign Sagittarius*

It is very rare that the Crab proves to be insensitive to the needs and wants of others, but this might be the case right now. It's not that you are being selfish – a word that doesn't really occur in your vocabulary. The fact is that you can't satisfy your own needs right now as well as please the world at large.

18 WEDNESDAY ☿ *Moon Age Day 14   Moon Sign Sagittarius*

Cancer is a Water sign, and like its sister signs, Scorpio and Pisces, it does have a fondness for luxury. Present trends enhance this, and there isn't much doubt that you will relish being comfortable. On the list of possibilities could be soaking in a long, luxuriant bath or cosseting yourself all evening.

19 THURSDAY   ☿ *Moon Age Day 15   Moon Sign Capricorn*

There is just a chance that you might fail to see the really important issues at the moment, particularly if you are dealing with so many routine chores. There are moments today when you need to surface from the dross and to see the sky shining above your head. Why not make a conscious decision to take an hour to yourself?

20 FRIDAY
☿ *Moon Age Day 16   Moon Sign Capricorn*

It's time to get new plans underway and also to examine facets of your life to see if you are carrying too much luggage around. Cancer isn't a Spartan sign, but you do sometimes get tied down by things that in the end are far from important. A lighter, less cluttered way forward should be possible with just a little imagination.

21 SATURDAY
Moon Age Day 17   Moon Sign Capricorn

If yesterday was somewhat difficult to negotiate, you can thank the lunar low, which is still having a bearing on your life today. For the moment you would be wise to continue your plans for the future, whilst at the same time avoiding making too many changes without taking time to ponder. A steady, family-motivated day would be no bad thing.

22 SUNDAY
Moon Age Day 18   Moon Sign Aquarius

The Moon now moves away from Capricorn, and you can rapidly get back to your old self. Every opportunity to either enjoy yourself or get ahead of the crowd in some way should be grabbed with both hands. If friends have need of you, they can be dealt with easily by giving them a little attention.

23 MONDAY
Moon Age Day 19   Moon Sign Aquarius

Getting along with specific individuals could be more complicated today – mainly because of the way you are feeling yourself. Don't be too quick to show a critical face to the world and accept the fact that you can be wrong on occasions. A high-handed attitude won't help at all, and might even get you into something of a fix.

24 TUESDAY
Moon Age Day 20   Moon Sign Pisces

What you can achieve today in terms of career development can be both interesting and ultimately financially rewarding. Maybe you will decide to go for a promotion, or else you have a good idea how to make something work out better for all concerned. Don't be afraid to talk to someone in the know, or even to approach your boss.

25 WEDNESDAY   *Moon Age Day 21   Moon Sign Pisces*

Even if you are still very business-minded, trends incline you today to go for the safe option. If you spoke out yesterday this needn't be a problem, because it means that people can see both sides of your nature. When it comes to your personal life there should be far less inhibition, and the Crab remains showy, sexy and powerful.

26 THURSDAY   *Moon Age Day 22   Moon Sign Pisces*

Your financial skill is now highlighted, as is your ability to impress people in a big way. Some Crabs may decide this is a good time to clean up their act, perhaps by giving up smoking or starting a healthier diet. Your present willpower is so strong that you could well succeed.

27 FRIDAY   *Moon Age Day 23   Moon Sign Aries*

Getting on side with fellow workers or friends is assisted by current trends, and your ability to co-operate is about as good as it gets. The Crab is sometimes a definite loner, but not at the moment. It is the stimulus you get from others that offers you the really good ideas that enable you to brighten your life no end today.

28 SATURDAY   *Moon Age Day 24   Moon Sign Aries*

Slight confusion about the way others are behaving is possible, and it would be quite sensible to double-check before you take any comment at face value. Even if it seems as if your natural perception is out of the window, this may not be the case at all. Perhaps everyone around you is acting as oddly as could be!

29 SUNDAY   *Moon Age Day 25   Moon Sign Taurus*

A little speculation might work well today, though you do need to be careful that you don't invest everything you have in one scheme that is, at best, risky. Rather you need to spread your efforts in a number of different directions and then you may well benefit from them all. Avoid any sort of pretence when dealing with your partner.

30 MONDAY   *Moon Age Day 26   Moon Sign Taurus*

You can take advantage of a great deal of energy as a new working week gets going, even if you are somewhat confused as to how you could best use it. In quieter moments you might have the chance to look back at a notion from the past. Even if it failed originally, prevailing circumstances could now be very different.

July

2008

1 TUESDAY
Moon Age Day 27 Moon Sign Gemin

Changes you can make in your financial situation could begin
offer you more in the way of security and a greater sense of bei
in charge of your own destiny. This in turn can lead to great
comfort in your surroundings, because you may decide that you c
afford to splash out on something that is entirely for the sake
luxury.

2 WEDNESDAY
Moon Age Day 28 Moon Sign Gemi

Your communication skills are to the fore, and you have scope
talk to anyone who comes along. As a result you can gather
number of different life stories, many of which carry object lesso
that are also applicable to you. The Crab is a good listener –
quality that enhances your life no end.

3 THURSDAY
Moon Age Day 0 Moon Sign Can

The lunar high at the beginning of July comes along at just the rig
time to offer a boost to most areas of your life. If things have be
too slow, you now have a chance to speed things up no end. M
important of all today is your ability to make a good impressi
when it matters the most. Be prepared to put yourself in
limelight.

4 FRIDAY
Moon Age Day 1 Moon Sign Can

Even if there are significant demands on your time today, you
cope very well with pressure and relish the prospect of pitting yo
wits against others. This might not be a time during which you
exactly move mountains, but it's worth having a very good try, a
in any case it is the impression you make on the way that count

114

SATURDAY
Moon Age Day 2   Moon Sign Leo

ou can now take decisive action to improve your personal finances
d might also be laying down plans that should see you better off
the longer-term future too. The Crab can be very courageous at
e moment and will stop at nothing to pursue a dream. Romantic
ertures are on offer, even if you don't expect them at all.

SUNDAY
Moon Age Day 3   Moon Sign Leo

ur home life is now more accented than has been the case for a
w weeks. Let's face it, you may have been very busy with life out
ere in the fast lane, but at the end of the day Cancer is a home-
d and the fact always shows out in the end. Today offers a chance
have your loved ones close to you.

MONDAY
Moon Age Day 4   Moon Sign Virgo

e focus is on caution at the beginning of this week, especially
en it comes to approaching others about favours you need. The
uble is that you prefer to do things for yourself if at all possible
d don't care for feeling obliged to anyone. However, there are
es when your best approach is to seek assistance from experts.

TUESDAY
Moon Age Day 5   Moon Sign Virgo

mulating new ideas and opportunities are there for the taking
und now, and if you are to make the best of either you need to
in the right frame of mind. Try to avoid getting bogged down
h tedious details or with jobs that leave you feeling numb from
neck up. Socially speaking you should be buzzing!

WEDNESDAY
Moon Age Day 6   Moon Sign Libra

ationships at home have potential to be very good at present,
that is the way you prefer things to be. If there's one thing that
Crab hates it's a lack of harmony around the homestead, so if
has been the case of late you can now make sure that things
le down. Colleagues can be quite inspirational today.

10 THURSDAY   *Moon Age Day 7   Moon Sign Libr*

It may be that personal attachments help greatly today when
comes to making up your mind about things. Maybe you shou
rely on the timely advice of your partner – someone who does, aft
all, have your best interests at heart. If friends have need of you
the moment, they might demand more time than you can offer.

11 FRIDAY   *Moon Age Day 8   Moon Sign Lib*

Make the most of a little material increase, which is possible no
that the Sun is in your solar first house. This is, after all, your mo
fortunate period of the year, even if it doesn't seem to be that w
on a moment-by-moment basis. Acting on impulse works be
today when you are faced with new social opportunities.

12 SATURDAY   *Moon Age Day 9   Moon Sign Scor*

Trends assist you to be better organised than might have been t
case across the last few days. Of course that may not help much
a work sense on a Saturday, but it could mean that you ha
everything shipshape at home. Once the chores are done, why r
find new ways to have some fun with friends?

13 SUNDAY   *Moon Age Day 10   Moon Sign Scor*

Your romantic side is highlighted, encouraging you to make a r
fuss of your partner. That's fine, just as long as they are r
preoccupied with something else. Don't get disappointed if you
to get the reaction you have been looking for – it's proba
nothing personal at all.

14 MONDAY   *Moon Age Day 11   Moon Sign Sagittar*

Even if there are great demands made on your energies at
moment, you should be more than ready to take them on, and w
is more you have spare capacity too. Avoid rows at work or w
friends and wherever it proves to be possible play the honest bro
It's a fine line though, because you could get drawn in.

5 TUESDAY   *Moon Age Day 12   Moon Sign Sagittarius*

Today is excellent for all communication matters, and you should have little or no difficulty in getting your message across to others. Routines can be a bit of a drag – though not if you leave a few of them to someone else to sort out. It's worth looking at family matters, because congratulations could be in order somewhere close.

6 WEDNESDAY *Moon Age Day 13   Moon Sign Sagittarius*

Your powers seem to be in the ascendant at the moment and especially so when it comes to influencing the thinking of those who are closest to you. This can best be achieved not by bulldozing but by gentle persuasion and dropped hints. When the true power of your nature is allied to all that diplomacy, how can you fail to win?

7 THURSDAY   *Moon Age Day 14   Moon Sign Capricorn*

A quieter time is on offer for the next couple of days, though there are such good planetary influences around you at present that the lunar low probably has little chance to slow you down dramatically. You may need to repeat jobs more frequently than would normally be the case.

8 FRIDAY   *Moon Age Day 15   Moon Sign Capricorn*

If you are still tending to take on ambitious goals, this might not be the best way forward, at least until tomorrow. Instead of pushing ahead too much at work today, your best approach is to clear the decks for actions you want to take later, whilst at the same time being willing to seek advice from colleagues who are in the know.

9 SATURDAY   *Moon Age Day 16   Moon Sign Aquarius*

Compromise is the key to success at home this weekend, though you may not be there very much. The summer weather, together with your own growing need for fresh fields and pastures new, could encourage you to set off on some sort of journey. However, it is not advisable to travel alone now if you want to have real fun.

20 SUNDAY
Moon Age Day 17   Moon Sign Aquari

The art of good conversation is really your forte at present, so i
worth actively seeking out interesting people so that you can ho
your verbal skills on them. A few family pressures could be
evidence, but such is your happy-go-lucky nature at the mome
that you can take these in your stride and shouldn't allow them
get in the way.

21 MONDAY
Moon Age Day 18   Moon Sign Aquar

Career moves that you choose to undertake at this time could w
take far less planning than you might have thought. The fact is th
if you are being watched carefully, you can make sure that those
positions of authority realise how much you are worth. This cou
put you in the driving seat when it comes to making progress.

22 TUESDAY
Moon Age Day 19   Moon Sign Pis

The focus is on independence under present trends, which is w
self-employed Crabs might prove to be the luckiest of all at t
moment. This would be an excellent time to take a break, and th
of you who have planned their holidays for this time could make t
an interlude to remember!

23 WEDNESDAY
Moon Age Day 20   Moon Sign Pis

There's no doubt about it, you have the personal touch at t
moment and since it would be a shame to waste all the hypno
power that is available, this might be the best time of all to ask
something you really want. It would probably take a very h
person to refuse you, and on the contrary, the most frequent wo
you hear now is yes.

24 THURSDAY
Moon Age Day 21   Moon Sign A

Trends suggest that you may have to take unexpected changes
your routines pretty much in your stride at present, and though t
can sometimes be slightly irritating, it shouldn't be much o
problem to most Crabs. The real fact is that anything that can sha
you out of pointless actions can be favourable in the end.

25 FRIDAY   *Moon Age Day 22   Moon Sign Aries*

Everyday dealings with the world at large should turn out to be quite pleasant, particularly if you choose to mix with informative and interesting people. Everyone has their story to tell, but you might be able to find out one or two now from people you never suspected were capable of being interesting.

26 SATURDAY   *Moon Age Day 23   Moon Sign Taurus*

It is important to remain realistic in your expectations just now. It would be too easy today to fly off at a tangent and to prepare yourself for something that really isn't very likely to happen. To do so might only lead to some disappointment further down the line, whereas if you expect very little you can make sure you end up delighted!

27 SUNDAY   *Moon Age Day 24   Moon Sign Taurus*

Planning is all-important when it comes to a project that has been close to your heart for a very long time. Others may well recognise your talent, and the moment is coming when you can prove the fact to yourself too. You are not top of the class when it comes to self-confidence, so anything that helps has got to be good.

28 MONDAY   *Moon Age Day 25   Moon Sign Gemini*

The tide of fortune is potentially starting to flow your way, though it happens at a fairly slow pace until the middle of the week and some patience is necessary if you are not going to get slightly disappointed with your own success. Your strength lies in moving slowly and steadily, whilst at the same time taking moments out to appreciate the summer.

29 TUESDAY   *Moon Age Day 26   Moon Sign Gemini*

There are signs that you need a change from routines and obligations, though it might be best to wait until tomorrow when trends will be going your way more than they are right now. Even if you are keen to get going today, there may well be something at the back of your mind that stops you – together with a mysterious lethargy.

30 WEDNESDAY   *Moon Age Day 27   Moon Sign Cancer*

Today is a time when you cannot only plan for the future, but have what it takes to put some of your plans into action. You have energy and determination in boatloads, together with a natural good luck that is unlikely to let you down when it really counts. Most important of all you can build up amazing popularity with others.

31 THURSDAY   *Moon Age Day 28   Moon Sign Cancer*

The tide of fortune continues to flow your way and you can make the best of the situation by being willing to take the odd chance. You needn't be short of the right sort of company because you should be able to attract winners at this time. Even someone you haven't cared for much in the past might be flavour of the month now.

August
2008

1 FRIDAY
Moon Age Day 0   Moon Sign Leo

You would be wise to think about what you are going to say before you open your mouth today. It isn't that you intend to offer any offence, simply that you speak before you have time to register the possible implications. Aside from the odd gaffe, you can get things to go your way, and romance is particularly well starred.

2 SATURDAY
Moon Age Day 1   Moon Sign Leo

A short journey could turn out to be just what the doctor ordered, and especially so if you undertake it with your partner. For those Crabs who are not attached in a romantic sense, this is definitely a good time to go out and actively seek a mate. A word of warning is necessary though – you needn't accept second-best just because its there.

3 SUNDAY
Moon Age Day 2   Moon Sign Virgo

It is towards the domestic side of life that your mind is now encouraged to turn, and there is nothing especially remarkable about that because it is often the chief concern of the Cancerian life. You won't mind a little drudgery this Sunday, even if others are constantly trying to get you out of the house and off on some journey.

4 MONDAY
Moon Age Day 3   Moon Sign Virgo

You have scope to give everyday discussions a slightly new feel now as you make the most of your increasing influence in certain directions. Use this wisely and try not to concentrate on too many matters at the same time. If you fail to use a little discretion you could end up in an unwanted argument.

5 TUESDAY
Moon Age Day 4   Moon Sign Virgo

What you can really show at present is how realistic you can be. This is partly down to little Mercury, which is now in your solar second house. Not only are you in a good position to sort out your own life, but you have what it takes to give some timely advice to both family members and friends. Colleagues may be less responsive.

6 WEDNESDAY
Moon Age Day 5   Moon Sign Libra

The focus is on financial improvements, so it's worth making sure you are giving money the attention it rightfully deserves. You have some ingenious ideas at present and needn't be at all reserved about sharing them with others, despite the fact that the Crab is sometimes inclined to hide its light somewhat.

7 THURSDAY
Moon Age Day 6   Moon Sign Libra

Strong ego energies could prevail today, and as a result you may not take kindly to people trying to correct you. This aspect has more of a practical than a personal application, so your love life and relationships in general should remain unaffected. Nevertheless you may be more easily upset than might normally be the case.

8 FRIDAY
Moon Age Day 7   Moon Sign Scorpio

Getting along in any sort of relationship doesn't have to be a battle. Others might not realise this fact, but you should. It's time to suppress the present tendency to defend yourself before you are attacked and to listen to what others are saying before you react. The more relaxed and easy-going Crab can once again prevail.

9 SATURDAY
Moon Age Day 8   Moon Sign Scorpio

Meetings with new individuals could prove to be quite pleasant and you are in a position to open yourself up to some unique situations. The fact is that you are curious about more or less everything and it is evident that you relish testing yourself in a number of different ways. Friendships could prove to be extremely important now.

10 SUNDAY   *Moon Age Day 9   Moon Sign Sagittarius*

The position of the Moon this Sunday offers you the chance to look again at specific actions you have been taking recently and to reassess how you should be reacting. You may have ideas about making a step up the career ladder, and today offers you some time to think about how best you should approach the matter.

11 MONDAY   *Moon Age Day 10   Moon Sign Sagittarius*

When it comes to getting ahead in a financial sense it is all down to good judgement, something that the Crab has in boat loads. Don't allow your decisions to be coloured by the opinions of others, and do whatever is necessary to get things going smoothly on the cash-flow front. This may require actions that are not universally liked.

12 TUESDAY   *Moon Age Day 11   Moon Sign Sagittarius*

You can remain generally confident, but it is worth noting that you have a couple of days in front of you that may be less positive. For that reason it would be sensible to get anything out of the way today that requires split-second timing or extra effort. This is particularly true in a career sense, but less so at home.

13 WEDNESDAY   *Moon Age Day 12   Moon Sign Capricorn*

It might be quite difficult today to get an objective picture of yourself or your actions, and as a result you may be tempted to take inappropriate actions. Better to do nothing at all than to march forward into situations that are only going to bring you problems later. Why not spend some time at home with family members and relish the chance of a break?

14 THURSDAY   *Moon Age Day 13   Moon Sign Capricorn*

Once again it might be better to put some plans on hold rather than to get everything wrong simply because you don't have what it takes to follow through. The lunar low is only around for today and there isn't much point in trying to swim against the prevailing tide. You can find plenty to do that is not remotely contentious.

15 FRIDAY
Moon Age Day 14   Moon Sign Aquarius

Now you can look ahead and plan your budget more effectively whilst at the same time showing a much more positive face to the world at large. The Sun remains in your solar second house, which enhances your objectivity and brings a time for building up your resources and working out how to spend very wisely.

16 SATURDAY
Moon Age Day 15   Moon Sign Aquarius

There may well be a few distractions about today, and since this influence is brought about by the position of the Moon, some of these might be emotional in character. Maybe your partner is behaving in a less than typical way, or it could simply be that you are more inclined than usual to take offence when none was intended.

17 SUNDAY
Moon Age Day 16   Moon Sign Aquarius

Venus is now in your solar third house and that turns out to be just right for mental inspiration. If you decide you need a change, this is an ideal time to get away from routines. Don't forget that this is August, and since some of those you know might be on holiday you can afford a break yourself.

18 MONDAY
Moon Age Day 17   Moon Sign Pisces

Mercury stands close to Venus in its own natural setting of the solar third house. This has to be extremely positive when it comes to communication, and you might even surprise yourself with your present eloquence. There could hardly be a better time than this during which to bring someone round to your point of view.

19 TUESDAY
Moon Age Day 18   Moon Sign Pisces

Financial powers are still in the ascendant and, all in all, this ought to turn out to be one of the most potent and useful periods of the year. Sometimes things just seem to slot into place and that is what you can make happen now. The Crab can even afford to back its own hunches – something it is often shy of doing.

20 WEDNESDAY   *Moon Age Day 19   Moon Sign Aries*

Get ready to rush ahead if necessary, and especially so when it comes to your work. You should not now miss out on any opportunity that presents itself and can move at lightning speed when you know it is necessary to do so. Even if you are busy now, you still have scope to support less-motivated friends.

21 THURSDAY   *Moon Age Day 20   Moon Sign Aries*

Even powerful Mars is now in your solar third house, though its position there is slightly less favourable than that of Mercury or Venus. There could be some tensions in your everyday environment and it may be difficult to keep things on an even keel. Most important of all, you would be wise to maintain your sense of humour.

22 FRIDAY   *Moon Age Day 21   Moon Sign Taurus*

If you keep your social life on a roll, this could bring emotionally uplifting experiences when they seem to matter the most. Although you might seem very cool to others, the Crab is often quaking a little inside. This is especially the case when you are put into the public eye. However, you can afford to be super-confident right now.

23 SATURDAY   *Moon Age Day 22   Moon Sign Taurus*

You benefit at the moment from a diversity of interests, which is one of the reasons why you might enjoy a holiday so much under prevailing trends. That might not be possible, but you can ring the changes no matter what your present circumstances. Even little alterations to your routines should seem like a sort of vacation.

24 SUNDAY   *Moon Age Day 23   Moon Sign Gemini*

Even if your general power to move mountains isn't quite as obvious today as you would wish, you are still more powerful and influential than you think. The Moon in your solar twelfth house might act as something of a blindfold, but you do have the ability to see past apparent obstacles and on towards ultimate successes.

25 MONDAY
Moon Age Day 24   Moon Sign Gemini

The saying goes, 'nothing ventured, nothing gained' and this is certainly true as far as you are concerned at the moment. The Moon has now moved into your solar third house and this assists you to keep your perceptions sharp and see what actions are most likely to work in your favour. You crouch – then you pounce!

26 TUESDAY
Moon Age Day 25   Moon Sign Gemini

For the third day in a row the Moon could act as something of a brake – not in a physical sense but with regard to the way you think. You may sense that something really good lies just around the corner but probably cannot see it for the moment. Patience is a virtue that the Crab has been given by providence, and now is the time to use it.

27 WEDNESDAY
Moon Age Day 26   Moon Sign Cancer

Today you could be like a coiled spring that has been released, because the lunar high allows all that pent-up energy to be discharged in an instant. A little faith and a good deal of optimism can go a long way, and you really do need to believe in yourself if you want to get the very best out of today. It's worth calling on the assistance of friends.

28 THURSDAY
Moon Age Day 27   Moon Sign Cancer

You have scope to make this a real red-letter day, and you shouldn't waste a minute in your quest for personal success and – surprise, surprise – personal glory. Even the Crab wants to be noticed sometimes and this proves to be the case under present trends. However, whether you will remain happy when in the limelight remains to be seen.

29 FRIDAY
Moon Age Day 28   Moon Sign Leo

Everyday matters should be both interesting and informative at the moment and can help you to embark on new projects with a great deal of confidence and a determination to succeed. Not everyone around you might share your present optimism, and if you have any task at all today it will be cheering up anyone who is down in the dumps.

30 SATURDAY
Moon Age Day 29   Moon Sign Leo

Ingenuity will be the key to success as far as money is concerned, particularly if you can somehow make a silk purse out of a sow's ear. Whatever you do, you need to remain positive as to the outcome of enterprises, and needn't be deterred by any deeply pessimistic types who are around just now.

31 SUNDAY
Moon Age Day 0   Moon Sign Virgo

It's the last day of August and should prove to be a marvellous time to be around the people you love the most. You can make this a very special day by showing how much you care. People are used to the Crab being affectionate, but the difference today is that you can find the time to prove the fact in a concrete way.

September
2008

1 MONDAY
Moon Age Day 1   Moon Sign Virgo

When it comes to communicating with others, today offers the best potential you could ever expect to encounter. However this won't be the case if you insist on hiding your light under a bushel, partly because you won't have much of interest to say. Now is the time to let your opinions flood out because they are far more welcome than you realise.

2 TUESDAY
Moon Age Day 2   Moon Sign Libra

Today responds best if you simplify things and take pleasure from domestic activities and even household chores. Life might have been getting just a little too hectic and complicated for some Crabs, so don't be afraid to apply the brakes. You need time to look at matters in greater depth.

3 WEDNESDAY
Moon Age Day 3   Moon Sign Libra

Happiness can be found in simple things right now and the beginning of September is peppered with opportunities for quiet moments of pleasure. Something as simple as a beautiful flower or a blood-red sunset can raise your spirits to fever-pitch in a way that very few other people could appreciate quite as you do.

4 THURSDAY
Moon Age Day 4   Moon Sign Scorpio

Mars has now moved into your solar fourth house, perhaps encouraging your moody side. This is not very common for the Crab, but of course everyone has periods when they are slightly out of sorts. If you realise the fact you can do something to counter it but those who care for you should understand anyway.

5 FRIDAY
Moon Age Day 5   Moon Sign Scorpio

You have scope to attract a great deal of affection from both expected and unexpected directions. You could even discover that you have an admirer you never suspected, and this might cause just a little embarrassment. Avoid getting bogged down with pointless details or boring jobs today.

6 SATURDAY
Moon Age Day 6   Moon Sign Scorpio

Relating to old friends and events from the past now seems to be second nature, which is fine just as long as you continue to appreciate that life is essentially about the present and the future. The Crab can sometimes be a little too nostalgic, and like all Water-sign individuals could begin to live in a sort of never-never land as a result.

7 SUNDAY
Moon Age Day 7   Moon Sign Sagittarius

A busy phase of communication is possible, but to the Crab that means listening as much as talking. Many of the conversations in which you take part could have hidden messages that will help you with your own plans for the future. Your job for today is picking these out from the background and working out how to proceed.

8 MONDAY
Moon Age Day 8   Moon Sign Sagittarius

The Moon in its present position supports efforts to follow through on recent proposals and possibilities, though without pushing too hard in new directions. Today can be quite steady and very useful, even if there is a certain lack of sparkle or excitement about it. Well, you can't always have cream cakes!

9 TUESDAY
Moon Age Day 9   Moon Sign Capricorn

It may feel as if you have to work harder at the moment to get anywhere, and for that you can thank the lunar low. This would not be a good time to push your luck or to force others into situations that don't appeal to them. In short, the less wake you make on your journey down the river of life today, the better you should feel.

10 WEDNESDAY *Moon Age Day 10   Moon Sign Capricorn*

There might be one or two unaccountable setbacks today, but nothing you can't cope with. Just don't try to do too much and be willing to allow others to take some of the strain for a while. There are gains to be made in the romantic department, particularly if you can make more time to concentrate on love right now.

11 THURSDAY *Moon Age Day 11   Moon Sign Capricorn*

For the third day in a row you begin the morning with the Moon in Capricorn. However, it will have moved on by just after lunch and that offers you scope to be more positive and anxious to get back on course after a few delays. By the evening you could well be raring to go, and might even decide to take a romantic chance.

12 FRIDAY *Moon Age Day 12   Moon Sign Aquarius*

If you keep your mental insights steady you should be able to focus intently on specific issues that you see being of paramount importance. There could be a few delays at first today but you can take those in your stride, and have what it takes to win through in the end if you adopt your patient Cancerian attitude.

13 SATURDAY *Moon Age Day 13   Moon Sign Aquarius*

Now is the time to speed things up and move closer to something you have been seeking for quite a while. Positive family news should help you to feel good on behalf of someone else. Don't allow yourself to get too tied down with irrelevant details or pointless tasks.

14 SUNDAY *Moon Age Day 14   Moon Sign Pisces*

The surprises are likely to continue and it is towards the social side of life that you are encouraged to turn at the moment. If doing the same old things time and time again doesn't appeal to you under present trends, your best response is to ring the changes in your search for happiness.

15 MONDAY
Moon Age Day 15   Moon Sign Pisces

Your ideas can have a great influence on the way those around you are behaving now, and you can make the new working week a positive time. Beware of getting too tied down with the needs of colleagues or friends, even if you really want to help. If you try too hard on their account at the moment you may hinder their progress.

16 TUESDAY
Moon Age Day 16   Moon Sign Aries

Along comes a potentially light-hearted time, courtesy of the planet Venus. Domestic relationships offer scope for some surprising and delightful experiences, whilst work issues are also favoured. Not all of your plans might work out as you wish, but you have what it takes to find suitable alternatives.

17 WEDNESDAY
Moon Age Day 17   Moon Sign Aries

Getting your head around priorities will be essential if you are to achieve your best today. If there is a problem around it is that there are too many things to do and only a certain amount of time available in which to do them. It's time to be selective and to get on with those tasks that you know to be of supreme importance.

18 THURSDAY
Moon Age Day 18   Moon Sign Aries

There are signs that your curiosity could be provoked today, and you will be able to enjoy yourself trying to find out all sorts of facts. Time spent at the computer or even at the local library would probably be worthwhile and you can certainly get your Sherlock Holmes hat on at the moment. Friends could be demanding but fun.

19 FRIDAY
Moon Age Day 19   Moon Sign Taurus

A sense of togetherness with close friends could help you to feel warm and comfortable, and you may decide to take some time out to have fun and to get together with people you have ignored recently. The more you laugh, the better you should feel, and you can find jokers around now to provide the giggles.

20 SATURDAY   *Moon Age Day 20   Moon Sign Tauru*

It looks as though self-determination is out of the window, for today
at least. You may well have to go down roads that are designated by
others and could even have to delay or abandon something you have
wanted to do. Be prepared to turn this into a positive thing by
maintaining a resolute attitude and staying cheerful.

21 SUNDAY   *Moon Age Day 21   Moon Sign Gemini*

You may decide this is a perfect time during which to take a break
from obligations. The month is growing older and it won't be too
long before the first chill winds of autumn are beginning to blow.
Make the most of any good weather that is still left in order to take
a break and to get out and about.

22 MONDAY   *Moon Age Day 22   Moon Sign Gemini*

By tomorrow things could be zinging, but for today you need to
plan. There are gains to be made from simply being in the right
place at the best time, and your instincts are unlikely to let you
down. However, the time is not yet quite right for speculation or
for taking on financial commitments that look doubtful.

23 TUESDAY   *Moon Age Day 23   Moon Sign Cancer*

Expect to be number one today and that is what you have a chance
to achieve. The lunar high should come at a very opportune time
and offers you more in the way of self-determination and a very
positive attitude to life. If you have been out of sorts of late, trends
assist you to get back to your old self.

24 WEDNESDAY   *Moon Age Day 24   Moon Sign Cancer*

When it comes to professional matters especially, there are signs that
you want to do things your own way and that you won't take no for
an answer. The Crab is usually so easy-going and quiet that on those
occasions when you really do show the force of your personality,
you can get others to fall in line without any argument at all.

25 THURSDAY ☿ *Moon Age Day 25 Moon Sign Leo*

It is towards home and domestic matters that your mind is now encouraged to return. This is a fairly common destination for the Crab, who is very family-orientated as a rule. It probably isn't that you feel unduly threatened by the outside world, more that you want to spend a greater proportion of your time with those to whom you feel closest.

26 FRIDAY ☿ *Moon Age Day 26 Moon Sign Leo*

A day to make yourself attractive to certain people, which is a positive thing if the feeling is mutual. Cancerians who are between romances at present should now be entering a much more positive phase, whilst those of you who are settled can find ways to pep up attachments, even if they are generally good.

27 SATURDAY ☿ *Moon Age Day 27 Moon Sign Virgo*

The pace of everyday events can now be increased, and present planetary trends are likely to offer the most potentially exciting weekend of September. Be prepared to make the most of invitations, and with everything to play for you should be particularly committed to romantic attachments, as well as relishing the company of friends.

28 SUNDAY ☿ *Moon Age Day 28 Moon Sign Virgo*

Strong emotional insights are to the fore at present, assisting you to be fully committed to loved ones and their needs of you. This strong 'giving' element is so much a part of the Cancer subject's makeup that it shows frequently. But as you give, so you will discover how much you are also getting.

29 MONDAY ☿ *Moon Age Day 29 Moon Sign Libra*

One thing you might seem to lack at the start of this new working week is self-discipline, which could make you feel less than comfortable, even though there may be little you can do about it in the short term. If you are in doubt about anything, now is clearly the time to seek the advice of people who are more qualified then you.

30 TUESDAY   ☿   *Moon Age Day 0   Moon Sign Libra*

Venus has now moved into your solar fifth house, helping you to elicit a warm response from others. There may be new romantic adventures on offer for some Crabs, together with a greater certainty that the attention you are giving someone very special will start to pay dividends. All in all today can be positive.

October

2008

1 WEDNESDAY   ☿   Moon Age Day 1   Moon Sign Libra

Since much depends at the moment on your feelings of domestic security, you may decide to devote a lot of your time to family matters at the beginning of October. There's nothing at all strange about this for you, because if you don't feel entirely happy with your home life, nothing else falls into place either.

2 THURSDAY   ☿   Moon Age Day 2   Moon Sign Scorpio

Strong creative tendencies start to appear and you need to turn your mind towards new incentives and ideas if things are not to grow a little stale. There are signs that your temper may be a little shorter than is usually the case, so beware of flying off the handle about matters that you would normally take in your stride.

3 FRIDAY   ☿   Moon Age Day 3   Moon Sign Scorpio

You can now express your caring nature in many different ways and have what it takes to make your nearest and dearest feel comfortable and happy. These favourable trends stay around you for most of the day, but if most of your thoughts are directed towards home, you might not be too professionally focused.

4 SATURDAY   ☿   Moon Age Day 4   Moon Sign Sagittarius

A socially uplifting time is available, and it arrives just in time for the weekend. The only slight problem comes for Crabs who work on a Saturday because this could prevent you from spending quite as much time enjoying yourself as you might wish. The secret is to find moments during which you can truly please yourself.

135

5 SUNDAY   ☿ *Moon Age Day 5   Moon Sign Sagittarius*

Although you may now suffer from a strong sense of urgency about everything you do, there is really no rush about today. On the contrary, the more careful you are to get things right, the less chance there is that you will have to do any of them again. If there are no social invitations coming in, why not think of something yourself?

6 MONDAY   ☿ *Moon Age Day 6   Moon Sign Sagittarius*

Get whatever you can done today in the knowledge that trends encourage a slow-down tomorrow and on Wednesday. It looks as though today is going to be good for all relationship issues and for getting on side with people around you who have real power. It's not a matter of luck, but rather good planning on your part.

7 TUESDAY   ☿ *Moon Age Day 7   Moon Sign Capricorn*

Some of your plans could now be thrown into reverse and although this is a very temporary state of affairs it might mean having to think again in some instances. Thinking is what you should be particularly good at right now, and you can still make progress, though by planning for the future rather than acting now.

8 WEDNESDAY   ☿ *Moon Age Day 8   Moon Sign Capricorn*

There's a potential double whammy to be dealt with today. If you get too confident when faced with issues that are going slightly wrong, you could end up making yet more mistakes. It is important to be as cautious as you can for the moment and to check and double-check all facts before proceeding in any direction.

9 THURSDAY   ☿ *Moon Age Day 9   Moon Sign Aquarius*

You can now get things back to normal, and can make use of your problem-solving skills today, not just for yourself but on behalf of others too. You will still need to be fairly exact in the way you measure any job or situation, but you do have a deep and penetrating intuition that is going to be of good use to you now.

0 FRIDAY ☿ *Moon Age Day 10* *Moon Sign Aquarius*

With the Sun in your solar fourth house between now and the 20th you may be especially drawn to home and family, which is not too surprising for the Crab at the best of times. Now is an ideal time to focus on how much other people mean to you, and on plans for your comfort during the upcoming winter.

1 SATURDAY ☿ *Moon Age Day 11* *Moon Sign Aquarius*

Don't be afraid to take your chances when it comes to romance, though of course you first have to realise that they exist. Some Crabs couldn't see a come-on if it jumped up and bit them, and that is because they don't feel themselves worthy of anyone else's affection. Why not use some confidence today?

2 SUNDAY ☿ *Moon Age Day 12* *Moon Sign Pisces*

There are strong mental lifts available today and you can use events to boost your confidence significantly. This would be a great time for getting out to the shops and finding a bargain. You may also be busy already planning for what the Christmas period is likely to have in store for you.

3 MONDAY ☿ *Moon Age Day 13* *Moon Sign Pisces*

It appears that you might want your own way in everything today, and that probably isn't going to be possible. Cancer is usually one of the most passive of all zodiac signs but there are indications that this might change a little today and tomorrow. Woe betide anyone who gets in your way or has the audacity to suggest you might be wrong!

4 TUESDAY ☿ *Moon Age Day 14* *Moon Sign Aries*

It's still a case of you believing you know almost everything, even if other people are doing their best to convince you that a contrary point of view might be valid. At least as today wears on you have a chance to rethink your position. There will be no shame in taking a u-turn if you know in your heart it is necessary.

15 WEDNESDAY ☿   *Moon Age Day 15   Moon Sign Arie*

Domestic life seems to be especially appealing under present trend
and you may decide that the time is right to retreat a little from th
world at large. Just like the creature for which your zodiac sign
named, there are times when you need to withdraw into your she
and to look at the world from within yourself.

16 THURSDAY   ☿   *Moon Age Day 16   Moon Sign Taur*

As a direct and rather speedy contrast to yesterday, you now hav
scope to show the strong social side of your nature and to mix an
mingle with any number of different people. This sudden change
attitude is influenced by the Moon, the quickest and mo
important planet as far as you are concerned.

17 FRIDAY   *Moon Age Day 17   Moon Sign Taur*

There could be a little confusion regarding personal plans, and
looks as though you will have to respond in an instant if you wa
to get the best out of most issues. Things are not helped if love
ones and friends have vacillating tendencies, and it might b
necessary for you to adapt quickly to their changing attitudes.

18 SATURDAY   *Moon Age Day 18   Moon Sign Gemi*

Today is especially favourable for all relationships, for which you ca
thank a fifth-house Venus. You have scope to get your own w
more than usual, and there shouldn't be much opposition to mo
of your plans. A few surprises are also possible, particularly if yo
seek a change of scenery.

19 SUNDAY   *Moon Age Day 19   Moon Sign Gemi*

You can afford to watch and wait, at least for the first part of the da
Even if you are straining at the leash to get on, it is tomorrow th
offers the best incentives. For today you need to be slightly mo
thoughtful and to weigh up the pros and cons of what lies befo
you. It is the cultured side of your nature that can be displayed no

20 MONDAY   *Moon Age Day 20   Moon Sign Cancer*

With the lunar high comes the time for putting fresh and innovative ideas to the test. Don't be shy about having your say and be willing to go that extra mile if that is what it takes to make people listen to you. You can now get Lady Luck to follow you around, though large-scale speculation still isn't advisable.

21 TUESDAY   *Moon Age Day 21   Moon Sign Cancer*

When it comes to planning ahead you are now second to none, and can achieve your fair share of successes right now. This is fairly dependent on self-belief, which you appear to have in cart-loads at the moment. When others see how confident you are they can be persuaded to follow your lead and suggestions.

22 WEDNESDAY   *Moon Age Day 22   Moon Sign Leo*

Venus has shifted its position, from the fifth to the sixth house. This supports smooth progress at work, together with a fairly laid-back attitude about potential changes. You can take new responsibilities in your stride and should be seeing ways to conquer fears from the past. This allows you to move forward in many ways.

23 THURSDAY   *Moon Age Day 23   Moon Sign Leo*

You can now make the most of your good ideas and bubbling enthusiasm. Almost anyone who comes your way today is grist to the mill of your curiosity and you may well be asking questions all day. The strangest things intrigue you and you now have a penchant for the odd or extraordinary.

24 FRIDAY   *Moon Age Day 24   Moon Sign Virgo*

What you are looking for at the moment – and in the main finding – is the opportunity to do your own thing. If routines are tedious, you may decide to shelve them or else leave them to others. Meanwhile you have what it takes to push forward, demonstrating your curiosity at every turn and enchanting your friends.

25 SATURDAY
Moon Age Day 25   Moon Sign Virg

Beware Mr or Miss Crab, because even if you insist on being ou there in the mainstream today, your usual charm may be eithe absent or else distinctly dulled. It appears that you retain a very hig opinion of yourself, which is fine, but what you don't have today quite the level of support from others you have come to expect.

26 SUNDAY
Moon Age Day 26   Moon Sign Virg

Demands that are made of you today could slow down you progress somewhat, and you might end up feeling fatigued if yo try to do too much. At least you can be your old self when it come to being able to please others and as a result help will be at han when you need it the most. Opt for a fairly quiet but still interestin Sunday.

27 MONDAY
Moon Age Day 27   Moon Sign Libr

If there are emotional ups and downs to be dealt with at the start this working week, the slight problem could be that you just don have the time to sort them out as you would wish. You need to tak a fairly matter-of-fact approach to life if you can, though this mig be rather difficult in the face of some awkward people.

28 TUESDAY
Moon Age Day 28   Moon Sign Libr

You can make sure your moment-by-moment dealings with othe are more pleasant today and can shine in all work and soci situations. Why not use your popularity to mix with others? Th only difficulty might be that you cannot be everywhere at onc Planning is required.

29 WEDNESDAY
Moon Age Day 0   Moon Sign Scorp

You have what it takes to attract just the right kind of help an support today, and can use it to answer thorny problems that ha been around for a while. This is especially true in the workplac where colleagues and superiors alike seem to be devoting most their time to assisting you.

30 THURSDAY   *Moon Age Day 1   Moon Sign Scorpio*

Boosts to your ego are now available through your love life, particularly if it is running smoothly. When it comes to the more practical aspects of life you need to take your time and to make sure that you do everything properly. Part of your present success comes from working and thinking in a tidy way.

31 FRIDAY   *Moon Age Day 2   Moon Sign Sagittarius*

Once again trends encourage you to organise yourself – and anyone else who is willing to listen to what you have to say. You want everything just so and although that's fine in the main, there might be one or two individuals who will kick against your present frame of mind. No problem – simply leave them alone!

November
2008

1 SATURDAY
Moon Age Day 3   Moon Sign Sagittariu

A day to enjoy being busy and active, and just about as chatty as
is possible for the Crab to be. Your present frame of mind has wh:
it takes to charm the birds down from the trees and you can also b
very funny at the moment, which everyone loves. In a person:
sense, avoid allowing anyone to give you the run-around.

2 SUNDAY
Moon Age Day 4   Moon Sign Sagittariu

Despite the potential for a few small problems at the start of the ne
working week, for today the sky looks blue – even if only in you
mind. You could benefit from a change of scenery and from th
chance to look anew at old situations. The presence of happy-g:
lucky friends can have a positive part to play in your thinking now.

3 MONDAY
Moon Age Day 5   Moon Sign Capricor

There could be a few minor disappointments to deal with toda
thanks to the arrival of the lunar low, but you needn't let these cau:
you much in the way of problems. In fact the planetary line-up is s
generally good at the moment that it's a fair bet that you can tur
the lunar low into at worst a neutral time this month.

4 TUESDAY
Moon Age Day 6   Moon Sign Capricor

If there are setbacks today it would be sensible to go with the flo
rather than trying to swim against the tide. Even if you feel capab
and quite determined at present, there isn't much point in trying t
recover situations that are lost. Better to concentrate on what yc
know you can achieve, though maybe not until tomorrow.

5 WEDNESDAY   *Moon Age Day 7   Moon Sign Aquarius*

Almost instantly you can now make a very favourable impression on just about anyone, with the help of powerful Mars, which presently occupies your solar fifth house. Prevailing trends could herald a little forgetfulness, so it's worth relying on welcome reminders from others.

6 THURSDAY   *Moon Age Day 8   Moon Sign Aquarius*

You may now decide to draw your horns in a little from a financial point of view, particularly if you sense that there are quite expensive times to come next month. All the same, this would not be a good way to make major purchases or to speculate wildly. Better by far to hang on to what you have for the moment.

7 FRIDAY   *Moon Age Day 9   Moon Sign Aquarius*

The focus is on the pursuit of fun and romance on this November Friday, so much so that work might go by the board for a few hours. Capricious Mercury now encourages mischief, and hones up your sense of the ridiculous. Why not persuade friends to join in the party?

8 SATURDAY   *Moon Age Day 10   Moon Sign Pisces*

If ever there was a good time for charming others into doing your bidding, that period is right now. You have a good sense of what you want from life and can easily identify the sort of people who can be of assistance. Once you have done so, pick the right approach in each case and hey presto, you should get what you need!

9 SUNDAY   *Moon Age Day 11   Moon Sign Pisces*

Now is the time to take advantage of a strong sense of personal freedom. You desperately need to do what appeals to you and probably won't take kindly to being bulldozed into any situation that goes against the grain. This is a Sunday that spells liberty for the Crab, and woe betide anyone who tries to tell you different.

10 MONDAY   *Moon Age Day 12*   *Moon Sign Arie*

All social issues are now well accented, though you may have som slight difficulty dealing with people in workplace situations. On th whole you would rather be off doing your own thing than havin to toe the line professionally, but you can find ways and means t mix business and pleasure in an enjoyable way.

11 TUESDAY   *Moon Age Day 13*   *Moon Sign Arie*

Trends assist you to move plans on the drawing board ahea towards a satisfactory conclusion, even if you have to put in a littl extra effort in some cases. You don't mind hard work at all at th moment, and can easily put your social aspirations on hold if i means working longer hours.

12 WEDNESDAY   *Moon Age Day 14*   *Moon Sign Tauru*

This is a very favourable time for all manner of informed discussion and for getting family members on your side. Not everyone may b quite so compliant, and this is particularly true in the case c colleagues and some friends. You need to pick your contacts carefull today and leave alone those who seem determined to be awkward.

13 THURSDAY   *Moon Age Day 15*   *Moon Sign Tauru*

Your strength now lies in getting partnerships to work well for you This includes personal attachments but is especially the case i business relationships and friendships that have a very practical sid to them. The Crab can also show its sporting side, and new interest could be coming along to captivate you.

14 FRIDAY   *Moon Age Day 16*   *Moon Sign Gemin*

The Moon now enters your solar twelfth house, a position fro which it encourages you to withdraw into yourself much more tha has been the case so far this month. If you aren't as approachable you have been, one or two people might be wondering what the have done to upset you. Now is the time to offer a little reassuranc

5 SATURDAY *Moon Age Day 17   Moon Sign Gemini*

quieter interlude is still indicated, though romantic matters look ositively highlighted. Today responds best if you leave practical sues more or less alone, in order to concentrate on what suits you est personally. By tomorrow you can fire on all cylinders in every spect.

6 SUNDAY *Moon Age Day 18   Moon Sign Cancer*

here is plenty of incentive for you to put the pedal to the metal day, and the only thing that might hold you back slightly is the ct that the lunar high occurs on a Sunday. This could restrict ofessional efforts but should do nothing to hold you back socially , more especially, in a romantic sense. Be prepared to tell it how is today.

7 MONDAY *Moon Age Day 19   Moon Sign Cancer*

is ought to be one of the best days of the month for putting new ans into operation and for getting them up and running. You no oner seem to start a task at present than it is finished, leaving you e to commence again somewhere else. This is a day for moving out as much as possible and for making a big impression.

8 TUESDAY *Moon Age Day 20   Moon Sign Leo*

ositive trends continue in the area of work and financial velopments. You can now achieve favourable results thanks to orts you made in the past. In particular you have what it takes to engthen your finances, and to keep this up in the months ahead.

9 WEDNESDAY *Moon Age Day 21   Moon Sign Leo*

easure can be placed high on your agenda today, and even if you l somewhat tied down by the practicalities of life you can find the ace for enjoyment if you put your mind to it. Friends can be rsuaded to join in and there are plenty of laughs in the offing for abs who are willing to give their best.

20 THURSDAY   *Moon Age Day 22   Moon Sign Le*

If you are not especially well organised today, an important pla
could go slightly wrong. It is the details of life that matter most fo
the moment and all your resources will be necessary to fine-tur
issues. There is absolutely no point in moving onto anything ne
until existing efforts are brought to fruition.

21 FRIDAY   *Moon Age Day 23   Moon Sign Virg*

Big things are possible on the romantic front, but once again it
necessary to get every detail right if you want to make the most ou
of any situation. You have scope to attract admirers, and to gai
compliments from a number of different directions under presen
planetary trends.

22 SATURDAY   *Moon Age Day 24   Moon Sign Virg*

It's time to focus squarely on particular tasks – a trend that h
shown up time and again across the last week. Now the accent
more squarely on your romantic life and what you can do to pep
up a bit. Socially speaking you should be more than ready to put c
your best clothes and to make a splash at any sort of gathering.

23 SUNDAY   *Moon Age Day 25   Moon Sign Libr*

If you are willing to rise to any challenge that comes your way yc
will make the most of all that is available at the moment. This is
Sunday that can offer a great deal, but you need to make yourse
available for everything. This isn't always easy for you because yc
sometimes show a little shyness and a worrisome nature.

24 MONDAY   *Moon Age Day 26   Moon Sign Libr*

Any intimate concerns and domestic matters that are on your mir
this Monday might take the edge off your professional capabilitie
though probably not for long. Even if life is working out fairly we
for you, you do need to concentrate more on issues that have bee
left rather on the shelf of late.

25 TUESDAY   *Moon Age Day 27   Moon Sign Scorpio*

Though personal matters may now be running less well for you, chances are that the reason lies beyond your own ability to control. Family upheavals and the strange behaviour of friends do little to help, and your best response is simply to remain positive.

26 WEDNESDAY   *Moon Age Day 28   Moon Sign Scorpio*

Issues in the practical world are well starred, which is more than can be said for domestic or friendship issues. All the more reason to buckle down and to get on with jobs that can be sorted out positively. Ordinary and everyday routines bring their own form of satisfaction and can help you to jog on towards your objectives.

27 THURSDAY   *Moon Age Day 29   Moon Sign Scorpio*

Stand by for a fairly frantic day – at least if you want to be on the receiving end of everything that looks good. You simply cannot get enough of life under present trends but if you are not careful you could end up losing out, simply because you are trying too hard. Today should be good for burying the hatchet regarding an old argument.

28 FRIDAY   *Moon Age Day 0   Moon Sign Sagittarius*

There is more potential power at your fingertips right now than has been the case for quite some time. The attitude of a friend could be surprising but at the same time enchanting, and you could discover that your recent efforts to please people are bearing definite fruit. You can increase your popularity as a result.

29 SATURDAY   *Moon Age Day 1   Moon Sign Sagittarius*

You have scope to get the best of both worlds today, if you get your practical and social lives working well. There are planetary highlights all round, together with a feeling that things are now going your way. Avoid too much self-satisfaction though, or you could be in for a slight shock.

30 SUNDAY   *Moon Age Day 2*   *Moon Sign Capricorn*

You would be wise to avoid scattering your energies on trivial matters today or the lunar low could take the wind out of your sails somewhat. Rather than diversifying too much, be prepared to do one job at a time and to complete it before you start on the next. Better still would be to take a complete rest and let others work.

December
2008

1 MONDAY
Moon Age Day 3   Moon Sign Capricorn

In a professional sense you could be missing out on some progress at the start of this week, and the lunar low doesn't do anything to help the situation. Even if others seem to be getting ahead better than you are, the best way to deal with this is probably to do nothing at all. Thinking is more appropriate for the moment.

2 TUESDAY
Moon Age Day 4   Moon Sign Capricorn

Be careful what you say and especially what you promise today. If you are inclined to panic more than usual, you could make all sorts of promises that you will have to come good on later. Instead of sticking your neck out, you would be far better off retreating into your shell and waiting for trends to improve tomorrow.

3 WEDNESDAY
Moon Age Day 5   Moon Sign Aquarius

Now you can make progress, especially on the work front. There are more in the way of new opportunities and the present position of the Sun sees things maturing according to plan. Your best approach is to keep your thought processes regular and sensible, and to seek positive attention from the direction of colleagues.

4 THURSDAY
Moon Age Day 6   Moon Sign Aquarius

Look out for a real enhancement to your love life as Venus takes up position in your solar seventh house. New romantic opportunities will be the way forward for some, but for all Crabs the social possibilities will also be better. Make use of every invitation that comes your way, even if you are a little shy on occasion.

5 FRIDAY
Moon Age Day 7   Moon Sign Pisces

It could be that practicalities demand a rather unusual or even unique approach today, and if you are very inventive at present that should not be a problem. Constantly trying to address issues in the same old way is not only boring, but it may not work too well. Stand by to impress colleagues and friends with your originality.

6 SATURDAY
Moon Age Day 8   Moon Sign Pisces

Why not use this period to widen your intellectual horizons. Virtually all Crabs are a good deal brighter than they think themselves to be and the fact should come home to you at present. Your strength lies in persuading others, especially family members, to adopt your ideas. A dose of 'Christmasitis' is possible today.

7 SUNDAY
Moon Age Day 9   Moon Sign Pisces

Today offers a chance to focus firmly on the impending festive season to make sure that everything will go off swimmingly. Cancer worries so much about its family that events like Christmas can sometimes be slightly spoiled by the fact. This time around you can afford to relax a little more.

8 MONDAY
Moon Age Day 10   Moon Sign Aries

Potential conflict is indicated by present trends. This is quite unnecessary and even if you are not the one to blame there is something you can do about the situation. It isn't your way to be bloody-minded or stubborn, but the planets seem to be encouraging this today.

9 TUESDAY
Moon Age Day 11   Moon Sign Aries

Success is now a case of being properly organised and it would be worthwhile taking some time out this morning to get things sorted out. If you don't, there is a good chance that specific plans will go wrong or that you will find yourself having to do the same thing over again. Forethought is definitely the key to success now.

10 WEDNESDAY   *Moon Age Day 12   Moon Sign Taurus*

The Moon will be moving into your solar twelfth house later today and that has potential to slow things down a little. If specific events seem to be moving at lightning pace it may be no bad thing. In the meantime you can only do your best to keep up and to also focus on a pressing personal matter that comes along.

11 THURSDAY   *Moon Age Day 13   Moon Sign Taurus*

Emotional support is now on offer, and you may be able to persuade relatives or your partner to support you much more than might have seemed to be the case recently. A lot of the difference is down to your own particular point of view, which is now more flexible. You can afford to be quite progressive today.

12 FRIDAY   *Moon Age Day 14   Moon Sign Gemini*

A day to get on with material issues and progress quickly towards your objectives, even if the attitudes of those around you make this more difficult than you might wish. Instead of getting frustrated about the fact, be prepared to laugh at the absurdity of life and to enjoy the social moments that are presented to you.

13 SATURDAY   *Moon Age Day 15   Moon Sign Gemini*

You are moving towards the lunar high for December but the Moon will not enter the sign of Cancer until the mid-afternoon. As a result this could be a very split day. Things might start out slowly but after lunch it may feel as though you are being shot out of a gun. Fortunately you have what it takes to cope with the sudden pressure.

14 SUNDAY   *Moon Age Day 16   Moon Sign Cancer*

One of your greatest qualities right now is your excellent judgement. Put this together with the progressive phase that is with you today and tomorrow and the recipe is one for greater success. Even if part of your mind is firmly set on Christmas, you have scope to think far beyond that period and well into the New Year.

15 MONDAY
Moon Age Day 17   Moon Sign Cance

This is the right time to get things done, and to rely on the goo offices of others to do even more on your behalf. If you use th general good luck that is on your side, you can afford to take a fev chances today. Be adventurous in your thinking and if it proves to b possible take some time out to do exactly what pleases you the mos

16 TUESDAY
Moon Age Day 18   Moon Sign Le

You may decide to work alone for the moment because that's whe you can concentrate the most. Unfortunately there is also possibility that people will keep interrupting you, and this leave you little choice but to address issues you would rather leave alon for the moment. The patience of the Crab needs to be present nov

17 WEDNESDAY
Moon Age Day 19   Moon Sign Le

It is important to stay focused in a practical sense, particularly there is a lot to be done. However, the present position of th Moon assists you to look ahead of yourself and encourages you t begin new experiments at this time. Some confusion could be th result, though there is a good deal of comedy possible too.

18 THURSDAY
Moon Age Day 20   Moon Sign Virg

Trends suggest that it's more a case of who you know than wha you know today, and you can help yourself greatly by simpl listening to what experts have to say. You have what it takes t improve joint finances at the moment, and though this might be strange time of year to plan how you can save money, some succes is possible.

19 FRIDAY
Moon Age Day 21   Moon Sign Virg

If you want real happiness today you may well be able to find it o those occasions when you are surrounded by many different type of people. You revel in diversity and can positively shine whe confronted with mysteries and paradoxes. Routines will probabl bore you, and your social life now depends on change and diversity

20 SATURDAY
Moon Age Day 22   Moon Sign Libra

Strangely enough the focus is now on a very deep sense of nostalgia. This is odd only in terms of the planets that have been predominating in your solar chart, but is not all that peculiar for the Crab as a rule. Perhaps there has been too much consideration of Christmas past and what it meant to you.

21 SUNDAY
Moon Age Day 23   Moon Sign Libra

Your approach to certain aspects of life may be somewhat rash and this will be especially likely if you work on a Sunday. Those Crabs who are at home can use up much of their energy in making sure that every detail is sorted out in the search for the most perfect festive season possible.

22 MONDAY
Moon Age Day 24   Moon Sign Scorpio

Social and love lives are both well accented at the start of this week and you may decide to take a few chances, especially at work. You feel quite balanced in your judgement and will continue to do so until someone tells you that you are about to make a very big mistake. It's worth listening to some advice.

23 TUESDAY
Moon Age Day 25   Moon Sign Scorpio

In partnerships, trends encourage you to look for kindred spirits, something that is presently just as applicable to professional relationships as to personal ones. You begin to sink into that famous Christmas spirit that is personified by the nature of the Crab, and if you haven't finished your decorations yet it will be a great surprise!

24 WEDNESDAY
Moon Age Day 26   Moon Sign Scorpio

You may have to alter your plans at the last minute, possibly because of someone else. This won't please you at all but there is enough flexibility in your thinking to make the changes necessary. Later on you can count a few hours as belonging to you, though even these you may decide to give away to the needs of Christmas.

25 THURSDAY   *Moon Age Day 27   Moon Sign Sagittarius*

It seems as though money could be on your mind at the moment, which is rather surprising on Christmas Day. Perhaps there is some cash coming your way in the form of presents or you are restructuring something in your mind. Now is the time for fun, and you have what it takes to persuade plenty of people to join in.

26 FRIDAY   *Moon Age Day 28   Moon Sign Sagittarius*

All relationships can be put under the spotlight to a certain extent on this Boxing Day and your strength lies in being open to opportunity and wise arguments. Some Crabs will be happy to travel under present trends and there isn't much doubt about your willingness to put yourself out wholesale for those you love.

27 SATURDAY   *Moon Age Day 0   Moon Sign Capricorn*

There is a three-day lull during the Christmas holidays, which comes about as a result of the lunar low. This time is best suited to relaxing and spending some time doing only those things that appeal to you. Why not lay off some of the socialising and catch up on all those books that came in your Christmas stocking?

28 SUNDAY   *Moon Age Day 1   Moon Sign Capricorn*

Hold-ups are possible, and your best response is to take on board what life is telling you and to react accordingly. Fortunately you can remain in a very mellow frame of mind at the moment, assisted by current planetary influences. Very little can touch you if you stay relaxed.

29 MONDAY   *Moon Age Day 2   Moon Sign Capricorn*

One-to-one relationships could bring a few disputes, even if these are not being directly caused by you. However, you probably won't take kindly to being told what to do and you can be quite stubborn at the moment if you are crossed in any way. Greater patience will be possible tomorrow, but for the moment just hang on.

30 TUESDAY   *Moon Age Day 3   Moon Sign Aquarius*

Today could be one of the best days of the month when it comes to social inspirations and pleasure in a general sense. Maybe you are able to relax more now that you know everything went the way you would have wished, or else you have abandoned any hope of making it do so. For whatever cause, the time is right to have fun.

31 WEDNESDAY   *Moon Age Day 4   Moon Sign Aquarius*

Success and satisfaction seem to be inextricably tied to personal attachments and to your home life as the year comes to its close. Nevertheless, if you have committed yourself to a very special sort of New Year's Eve, you can help others to enjoy themselves too. That's the way of the Crab and it won't change.

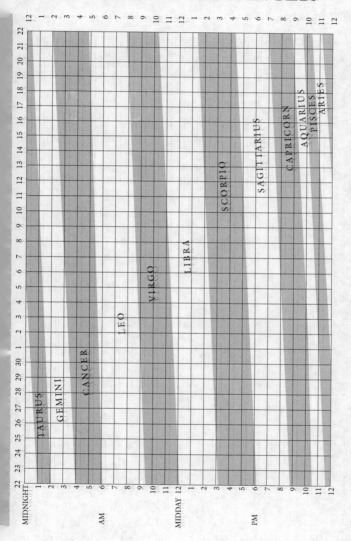

THE ZODIAC, PLANETS AND CORRESPONDENCES

The Earth revolves around the Sun once every calendar year, so when viewed from Earth the Sun appears in a different part of the sky as the year progresses. In astrology, these parts of the sky are divided into the signs of the zodiac and this means that the signs are organised in a circle. The circle begins with Aries and ends with Pisces.

Taking the zodiac sign as a starting point, astrologers then work with all the positions of planets, stars and many other factors to calculate horoscopes and birth charts and tell us what the stars have in store for us.

The table below shows the planets and Elements for each of the signs of the zodiac. Each sign belongs to one of the four Elements: Fire, Air, Earth or Water. Fire signs are creative and enthusiastic; Air signs are mentally active and thoughtful; Earth signs are constructive and practical; Water signs are emotional and have strong feelings.

It also shows the metals and gemstones associated with, or corresponding with, each sign. The correspondence is made when a metal or stone possesses properties that are held in common with a particular sign of the zodiac.

Finally, the table shows the opposite of each star sign – this is the opposite sign in the astrological circle.

Placed	Sign	Symbol	Element	Planet	Metal	Stone	Opposite
1	Aries	Ram	Fire	Mars	Iron	Bloodstone	Libra
2	Taurus	Bull	Earth	Venus	Copper	Sapphire	Scorpio
3	Gemini	Twins	Air	Mercury	Mercury	Tiger's Eye	Sagittarius
4	Cancer	Crab	Water	Moon	Silver	Pearl	Capricorn
5	Leo	Lion	Fire	Sun	Gold	Ruby	Aquarius
6	Virgo	Maiden	Earth	Mercury	Mercury	Sardonyx	Pisces
7	Libra	Scales	Air	Venus	Copper	Sapphire	Aries
8	Scorpio	Scorpion	Water	Pluto	Plutonium	Jasper	Taurus
9	Sagittarius	Archer	Fire	Jupiter	Tin	Topaz	Gemini
10	Capricorn	Goat	Earth	Saturn	Lead	Black Onyx	Cancer
11	Aquarius	Waterbearer	Air	Uranus	Uranium	Amethyst	Leo
12	Pisces	Fishes	Water	Neptune	Tin	Moonstone	Virgo

THE ZODIAC, PLANETS AND CORRESPONDENCES